The Founding Fathers' Guide to the Constitution

The Founding Fathers' Guide to the Constitution

BY BRION McCLANAHAN

REGNERY
HISTORY

Library of Congress Cataloging-in-Publication Data

McClanahan, Brion T.
  The Founding Fathers' Guide to the Constitution / Brion McClanahan.
    p. cm.
  ISBN 978-1-59698-193-5 (hardback)
  1. Constitutional history--United States. 2. United States. Constitutional Convention (1787) 3. Founding Fathers of the United States. I. Title.
  KF4541.M335 2012
  342.7302'9--dc23

                              2011020735
Published in the United States by
Regnery Publishing, Inc.
One Massachusetts Avenue, NW
Washington, DC 20001
www.regnery.com
Manufactured in the United States of America
10 9 8 7 6 5 4 3 2 1
Books are available in quantity for promotional or premium use. Write to Director of Special Sales, Regnery Publishing, Inc., One Massachusetts Avenue NW, Washington, DC 20001, for information on discounts and terms or call (202) 216-0600.

Distributed to the trade by
Perseus Distribution
387 Park Avenue South
New York, NY 10016

To my children

Contents

Introduction

Both the Left and Right claim the Constitution and its meaning as their own. Leftists like to cite the "elastic" clauses of the Constitution while conservatives often call it a "limiting" document. But how did the founding generation view the document, particularly when it was being sold to the States for ratification? What did the Preamble mean to them? How did they define the powers of Congress, the president, and the federal court system? And what about the so-called "elastic" or "sweeping" clauses of the Constitution? Does the Left have a case, or is the Constitution a "limiting document" as the Right suggests? The battle over the Constitution and its meaning cuts to the heart of the United States polity.

The story of how the Constitution came to be is well told. Following the American War for Independence, the central government under the Articles of Confederation proved too "weak" to handle the tasks of the Union. There was internal discord (particularly in Massachusetts), State paper currency was worthless, taxes were too high, treaties were unenforceable, and the commercial relationships between several States were strained at best. The Union seemed to be in peril and open to a foreign invasion. As a result, several leading men in the States—Alexander Hamilton and James Madison foremost among them—advocated calling a convention to discuss changes to the Articles.

They first met at Annapolis in 1786, but delegates from only five States showed up, and they were powerless to make any substantial recommendations to the United States Congress. They instead called for a new convention to meet in Philadelphia in May 1787 under the guise of amending the Articles of Confederation. Fifty-five men from eleven States attended, among them some of the most distinguished names in American history, including George Washington and Benjamin Franklin. Many were shocked to learn that Madison and Hamilton did not want to amend the Articles, but instead wished to start over with a new governing document. Madison, through fellow Virginian Edmund Randolph, presented the famous "Virginia Plan" to the Convention in the opening week. This plan scrapped the Articles, created a new "national" government with "supreme" legislative, executive, and judicial branches, and truncated the powers of the States. For his part, Hamilton preferred that the States be abolished altogether and advocated that both the executive and the members of the upper house in the "national" congress be elected for life. Neither Hamilton nor Madison would have his wish, and the document they would be forced to defend during the ratification process barely resembled the ambitious plans each man wanted when the Convention began.

During that hot summer in 1787, the members of the Philadelphia Convention hammered out in secret deliberations what Catherine Drinker Bowen called the "Miracle at Philadelphia."[1] The end result was a document littered with compromises, the most important being one between the "small States" and "large States." Everyone at that time, however, knew that those terms were nothing more than code words for a "national" centralized government versus a "federal" decentralized government. *That* part of the story is often omitted, but it was the real battle. As the Constitution moved to the States for ratification, the great debate was whether we should have a national or a federal government. The Constitution created a stronger central authority, as its proponents wanted, but it also had limits—and it was the central government's limits that were sold to an otherwise reluctant public. Most Americans would not have accepted ratification had the Constitution not been presented as a plan for a strictly limited government. That is the key to understanding the Constitution.

Some say the Constitution cannot be understood at all. In December 2010, liberal columnist Ezra Klein said, "The issue of the Constitution is that the text is confusing because it was written more than 100 years ago, and what people believe it says differs from person to person and differs depending on what they want to get done."[2] Just three months earlier, historian and author Ron Chernow suggested that because the founding generation never agreed on anything, a "founding interpretation" of the Constitution is impossible.[3] But neither of these critiques is right.

Certainly, Chernow is correct that the founding generation vigorously debated the meaning of the Constitution, particularly when it was sent to the States for ratification. But, in contrast to his assertion that Americans cannot arrive at a "founding interpretation," a clear consensus can be gleaned from these debates. We know how the founding generation interpreted the various provisions of the Constitution because we can read what they said. The Constitution is not ambiguous or difficult to understand. Of course, the trappings of power and, at times, practical political problems altered views of the Constitution, even in the founding generation, but this did not change the meaning of the Constitution *as ratified*. The record is clear. The way proponents of the document *defended* it is the way it should be interpreted. Unfortunately for men like Klein and Chernow, that interpretation does not often mesh with their vision for American government. It never has for progressives.

A few definitions are in order. Which of the "Founding Fathers" are included in *The Founding Fathers' Guide to the Constitution*? The answer is simple: all of them. In addition to James Madison and Alexander Hamilton—the two members of that generation who, because of the *Federalist Papers,* are often cited as the "true" expositors of the document—others, such as James Wilson, Patrick Henry, Luther Martin, Roger Sherman, Elbridge Gerry, George Mason, William Richardson Davie, James Iredell, Oliver Ellsworth, Melancton Smith, John Dickinson, Charles Pinckney, John Rutledge, and Robert Whitehill, are frequently cited for their contributions to the debate. Some were both members of the Philadelphia Convention of 1787 and their State ratifying conventions. Others took part only in their State conventions, and others, such as Tench Coxe and Richard Henry Lee, took part in neither but provided critique and analysis of the Constitution and its provisions. They were all part of the debate over ratification and, as such, it was *their* Constitution.

The common terms "Federalist" and "Anti-federalist" are not found in this book; instead I've substituted the terms "proponents" and "opponents" respectively. Opponents of the Constitution were never comfortable with the term "Anti-federalist." They correctly pointed out during the ratification debates that what they wanted was to *retain* the federal system of the Articles of Confederation, and the proponents of the Constitution, instead of being federalists, were in fact nationalists bent on eliminating the State governments. Elbridge Gerry of Massachusetts remarked in 1789 that "those who were called antifederalists at the time complained that they had injustice done them by the title, because they were in favor of a Federal Government, and the others were in favor of a national one; the federalists were for ratifying the constitution as it stood, and the others not until amendments were made. Their names then ought not to have been distinguished by federalists and anti-federalists, but rats and antirats."[4] This colorful description may be tinged by the politics of his day, but Gerry was on to something. Our modern conception of how the Constitution was argued and ratified has also been distorted by the way the *winning* side framed the debate. This work takes the other side seriously.

In fact, the way the winning side described the Constitution has led to perhaps one of the greatest misnomers in American history. Rather than use the term "federal" to describe the government created by the Constitution, this book replaces it with "general" or "central" as the founding generation described it. The government was constituted for the "general" purposes of the Union and, as opponents argued, it had only one "federal" component in the original document, the Senate. However, because of the Seventeenth Amendment to the Constitution, that no longer holds true. The government under the Constitution has always been "general" or "central," but never "federal."

The best way to "discover" the Constitution *as ratified* is to read the words of the men who wrote it and ratified it in 1787 and 1788. This work relies upon those words rather than the lofty and often deceptive interpretations written by historians who "think" they know what the Founders meant. Along with a virtual clause-by-clause discussion of the Constitution, the book also provides an extensive appendix containing quotations that provide context about particular points of interest and a list of proposed amendments that Madison eliminated in his final draft of the Bill of Rights. These are as important as the text itself. Ultimately, the Constitution should be read and understood the way the founding generation read and understood it in 1787 and 1788. Regardless of what men like Klein and Chernow think, that can be done.

CHAPTER 1

The Preamble

"We the People of the United States, in Order to form a more perfect Union, establish Justice, insure domestic Tranquility, provide for the common defense, promote the general Welfare, and secure the Blessings of Liberty to ourselves and our Posterity, do ordain and establish this Constitution for the United States of America."

Short of Thomas Jefferson's famous lines from the Declaration of Independence, the Preamble to the Constitution is perhaps the most famous fifty-two words in American history. Every schoolchild is required to memorize it; every American knows at least

the first seven words, and "We the people of the United States …"
is cited in part or whole by Americans on a daily basis as a declaration of their role in the government. It is "their" government
because the Constitution says so. But most Americans don't know
what the Preamble meant to the founding generation (or what it
means to the Constitution), the different version that existed before
the final draft of the Constitution was written, or the fact that it
was vehemently opposed by various individuals from the founding
generation during the State ratification process.

A preamble is a declaration of intent. It outlines the proposed
document in broad strokes, but it has no legal value and is not a
declaration of rights or liberties. So, while Americans hold the
Preamble to the Constitution as sacred, and while it is a beautifully
written and meaty fifty-two words, its overall value to the document, short of "setting the stage," is limited.

In fact, most Americans don't realize that the first drafts of the
Constitution contained the following preamble, written by nationalist Charles Pinckney of South Carolina, for the "free and independent states of America":

> We the People of the States of New-Hampshire, Mas-
> sachusetts, Rhode-Island and Providence Plantations,
> Connecticut, New-York, New-Jersey, Pennsylvania,
> Delaware, Maryland, Virginia, North-Carolina, South-
> Carolina, and Georgia, do ordain, declare and establish
> the following Constitution for the Government of Our-
> selves and our Posterity.[1]

The Committee of Style, led by New Yorker Gouverneur
Morris, changed the text of the Preamble and presented it to the

Philadelphia Convention at large on 12 September 1787, only five days before the Constitution was signed. Morris condensed the various objectives for a new government that had been discussed in Philadelphia, and eliminated the roll-call of States, perhaps because Rhode Island did not send delegates to the Convention. No discussion ensued over Morris's changes to the Preamble and historians have debated his intent.

Morris was generally a nationalist, but he recognized the sovereignty of the States—particularly when he favored the secession of the New England States in 1815—and advocated voting on the Constitution by State rather than by individual delegate on the final day of the Convention. Of course, the Preamble would be a subject of debate in the months and years after the Constitution was signed. These fifty-two words went to the heart of the debate over the Constitution: would the United States be a federal republic—that is, a confederation of sovereign States—or a consolidated nation? Some supported the language of the Preamble, others opposed it; James Madison chided those who sought to read more into it than was actually there.

Patrick Henry, the most dominant political figure in the State of Virginia and possibly the best orator in the United States, asked in the Virginia Ratifying Convention, "My political curiosity, exclusive of my anxious solicitude for the public welfare, leads me to ask, Who authorized them to speak the language of *We, the people*, instead of, *We, the states?* States are the characteristics and the soul of a confederation. If the states be not the agents of this compact, it must be one great, consolidated, national government, of the people of all the states."[2] Robert Whitehill of Pennsylvania, a strong-willed backcountry Scotch-Irish opponent of the Constitution, determined that the Preamble left no doubt about the intentions of the Framers. "We the People of the United States is a sentence that evidently shows the old foundation of the Union is destroyed, the principle of confederation excluded, and a new system of consolidated empire is set up upon the ruins of the present compact between the states."[3] Samuel Adams, the famous Patriot from Massachusetts, wrote in 1787 that the Preamble pointed to one conclusion. "I meet with a National Government, instead of a federal Union of Sovereign States...."[4] And "Brutus," possibly the most famous opponent of the Constitution, because of his detailed essays against it, wrote that "it is not an union of states or bodies corporate; had this been the case the existence of the state governments, might have been secured. But it is a union of the people of the United States considered as one body, who are to ratify this constitution, if it is adopted."[5]

Proponents of the document did not understand the critique. James Wilson, the most vocal defender of the Constitution in Pennsylvania and maybe the United States, responded to several critics of the Preamble's language in the Pennsylvania Ratifying Convention. "We the People—it is announced in their name, it is clothed with their authority, from whom all power originated and ultimately belong. Magna Carta is the grant of a king. This Constitution is the act of the people and what they have not expressly *granted*, they have *retained*."[6] "A Native of Virginia," probably Daniel Fisher, argued in 1788 that "the introduction, like a preamble to a law, is the key of the Constitution. *Whenever federal power is exercised, contrary to the spirit breathed by this introduction, it will be unconstitutionally exercised, and ought to be resisted by the people*"[7] (emphasis added). Edmund Randolph, the dashing lawyer and later governor of Virginia who presented Madison's Virginia Plan in the Philadelphia Convention, emphasized, "The

Government is for the people; and the misfortune was, that the people had no agency in the Government before [under the Articles of Confederation]."⁸ The Preamble, he said, made that clear. "Chancellor" Robert R. Livingston of New York, a member of the committee of five that drafted the Declaration of Independence and a very well-respected man in his State, thought that the language of the Preamble actually strengthened liberty and peace among the States.

> It has pleased Heaven to afford the United States means for the attainment of this great object [peace], which it has with-held from other nations. They speak the same language, they profess the same religion; and, what is of infinitely more importance, they acknowledge the same great principle of government ... *that all power is derived from the people.* They consider this State, and their general governments, as different deposits of power. In this view, it is of little moment to them whether that portion of it, which they must for their own happiness lodge in their rulers, be invested in the State Government *only*, or shared between them and the council of the Union. The rights they reserve are not diminished, and probably their liberty acquires an additional security from the division.⁹

Madison, however, had the final word on the controversy. Writing years after the ratification of the Constitution, he contended, "The general terms or phrases used in the introductory propositions, and now a source of so much constructive ingenuity, were never meant to be inserted in their loose form in the text of the

Constitution. Like resolutions preliminary to legal enactments it was understood by all, that they were to be reduced by proper limitations and specifications, into the form in which they were to be final and operative; as was actually done in the progress of the session."[10] There it is. Madison believed the Preamble was nothing more than a "preliminary" or "introductory propositions" limited by the text of the document itself. Reading between the lines was contrary to its meaning.

The argument that Morris truncated the original preamble to avoid confusion should some States not ratify the Constitution holds weight. He manifestly did not intend for the Union to be a consolidated mass of one people—his public career argued against that point; as Edmund Randolph pointed out, Morris merely wanted to ensure, in contrast to the Articles of Confederation, that the people were explicitly recognized in the Constitution, nothing more, nothing less.

Ultimately, the Preamble echoed Jefferson's language in the Declaration of Independence when he wrote that "it is the right of the people to alter or abolish it [government], and to institute new government, laying its foundation on such principles, and organizing its powers in such form, as to them shall seem most likely to affect their safety and happiness." This sovereignty of the people to make and unmake governments was what Morris affirmed. It was also the understanding of the States that ratified the Constitution, and that, really, is the key point. As Madison consistently advocated in his private letters, the Constitution should be supported the way it was *ratified*: the meaning of the Constitution, he wrote, is to be found "*in those of the State Conventions which gave it all the validity & authority it possesses*"[11] (emphasis added). The Preamble should be understood as an introduction to what the Founders, in their ratifying conventions, thought the federal government should be.

CHAPTER 2

The Legislative Branch

During a March 2010 town hall meeting in New Jersey, Representative Frank LoBiando of New Jersey's Second Legislative District was asked to explain Article I, Section 1 of the Constitution. He replied that Article I, Section 1 guaranteed Americans free speech. His response is a classic example of how little most Americans, even those who take an oath to defend and uphold the Constitution, know what is in the document. Of the seven Articles in the Constitution, Article I is the most important. Divided into ten sections, it establishes the legislative branch, defines the nature of the general government and its relationship vis-à-vis the States, and enumerates its powers. It received the most attention during the ratification debates of 1787 and 1788 and contains some of the most contentious clauses in the Constitution.

Section 1 declares, "All legislative powers herein granted shall be vested in a Congress of the United States, which shall consist of a Senate and House of Representatives." This bicameral system was a fundamental change to the Articles of Confederation and is the key to the general government. By design, the only "national" and "democratic" element of the Constitution is the House of Representatives. The Framers intended the Senate to retain the federal nature of the government under the Articles, in which each State had an equal vote in the Congress. William Richardson Davie of North Carolina, a member of the Philadelphia Convention and an ardent supporter of the Constitution, reasoned during the North Carolina Ratifying Convention of 1788 that "steadiness and wisdom are better insured when there is a second branch, to balance and check the first." That second branch (the Senate) represented "the sovereignty of the states," while the House of Representatives relied on the "broad basis of the people." In fact, he asserted that "the state governments are the pillars upon which this government is extended over such an immense territory, and are essential to its existence."[1] His view comported with those of the majority of the Founding Fathers, particularly in relation to a general distrust of democracy and the importance of the "sovereignty of the states."

The House of Representatives

Elbridge Gerry famously said in the opening days of the 1787 Philadelphia Convention, "The evils we experience flow from the excess of democracy."[2] While much of the Convention agreed, most thought that at least one house in the new government ought to be directly elected by the people. The end result was the House of Representatives. Article I, Section 2 states that "the House of Representatives shall be composed of Members chosen every second Year by the People of the several States." Every member of the House has to be at least twenty-five, a citizen of the United States for at least seven years, and an "Inhabitant of that State in which he shall be chosen."

As William Pierce of Georgia noted during the Convention, the House represents Americans as individuals, but the States still have a role. Members have to be residents of the States in which they are chosen and the States set "the Qualifications requisite for Electors of the most numerous Branch of the State legislature." In other words, the House of Representatives could not exist without the States because the States set both the elections and qualifications for office. As Alexander Hamilton said in 1788, "While the Constitution continues to be read, and its principles known, the states must, by every rational man, be considered as essential, component parts of the Union."[3]

Madison's Virginia Plan called for both houses in the new government to be based on proportional representation. In essence, the larger and more populated States would have had a greater role in the government. This was rejected in part because the small States feared they would be swallowed up by the large States but also because several members of the Convention—from both small and large States—rightly saw this as a means for consolidation of the government. Thus, in a compromise hammered out by Roger Sherman of Connecticut, the House of Representatives would be based on proportional representation while the Senate would be composed of two representatives from each State. Determining the final proportion, however, would be a substantial issue both during the Convention and in the State Ratifying Conventions.

Article I, Section 2, Clause 3 originally set the proportion of people to their representatives at 30,000 to 1. "Representatives and direct Taxes shall be apportioned among the several States which may be included within this Union, according to their respective Numbers.... The Number of Representatives shall not exceed one for every thirty Thousand, but each State shall have at Least one Representative...." Early drafts of the Constitution had the ratio as high as 40,000 to 1 (or simply apportioned by State, meaning that each State would be allotted a set number of seats), but in the final days of the Convention, Nathanial Gorham of Massachusetts and George Washington recommended that the ratio be reduced. Washington argued that 40,000 to 1 did not secure the "rights and interests of the people."[4] Still, many in the founding generation thought the final 30,000 to 1 ratio did not protect the people from the government or secure adequate representation. This was particularly true in the important States of Pennsylvania, New York, and Massachusetts, where both the ratio and term length for members of the House were questioned.

New Yorker Melancton Smith, a firm opponent of the Constitution, contended that a ratio of 30,000 to 1 excluded the "respectable yeomanry" from the government and opened the possibility of "corruption and combination." He said, "A great politician has said that every man has his price. I hope this is not true in all its extent; but I ask the gentleman [Alexander Hamilton] to inform me what government there is in which it has not been practiced." Smith then reasoned that with the initial number of ninety-one members of the Congress—twenty-six senators and sixty-five representatives— twenty-four men could control the government through a quorum and simple majority. "Can the liberties of three millions of people be securely trusted in the hands of twenty-four men? Is it prudent to commit to so small a number the decision of the great questions which will come before them? Reason revolts at the idea."[5] Writing as "Cato," New York Governor George Clinton suggested that the government could not "resist the influence of corruption, and the temptation to treachery" with so few members in the House.[6]

The minority of the Pennsylvania Ratifying Convention agreed. On 18 December 1787, the group, led by Robert Whitehill, John Smilie, and William Findley, published the "Dissent of the Minority of the Convention" in Pennsylvania newspapers. They challenged the ratio of 30,000 to 1 and were suspicious that the number of representatives in the House would be increased to meet the needs of the people. "Thus it appears that the liberties, happiness, interests, and great concerns of the whole United States may be dependent upon the integrity, virtue, wisdom, and knowledge of 25 or 26 men. How inadequate and unsafe a representation! Inadequate because the sense and views of 3 or 4 millions of people diffused over so extensive a territory comprising such various climates, products, habits, interests, and opinions cannot be collected in so small a body." They also contended that "the number of representatives will probably be continued at 65, although the population of the country may swell to treble what it now is; unless a revolution should effect a change."[7]

The Ratifying Convention of Massachusetts spent three days on the issue of representation. Dr. John Taylor thought the "House of Representatives was too small." In fact, he pointed out that sixty-five was a 30 percent reduction of the number of representatives under the Articles of Confederation. He believed that a large representative body was not "unwieldy" and used the Massachusetts House of Representatives and its 150 members as a fine example of good government.[8]

This charge was repeated in State ratifying conventions and in the press with some effect, so much so that proponents of the Constitution had to continually defend the design of the House. In Massachusetts, Francis Dana countered both Taylor, on the issue of representation, and opponents, who insisted that the Constitution destroyed the States. "If the Constitution under consideration was in fact what its opposers had often called it, a consolidation of the states, [I] should readily agree with that gentleman [Taylor] that the representation of the people was too small." But, he asserted, "it must be apparent to every one, that the federal government springs out of, and can alone be brought into existence by, the state governments. Demolish the latter, and there is an end of the former.... Besides, this representation will increase with the population of the states, and soon become sufficiently large to meet that gentleman's ideas."[9]

James Wilson of Pennsylvania explained that the Framers "endeavored to steer a middle course" in setting the ratio at 30,000 to 1. "Permit me to add a further observation," he said during the State Ratifying Convention, "that a large number is not so necessary in this case as in the cases of state legislatures. In them there ought to be a representation sufficient to declare the situation of every county, town, and district.... But in the general government, *its objects are enumerated*, and are not confined, in their causes or operations, to a county, or even to a single state"[10] (emphasis added). Wilson suggested that the powers of the federal government were "confined" to general issues and thus a smaller body of representatives were adequate for "general" purposes.

Madison addressed the issue in five of the Federalist essays, and argued in Federalist No. 58 that a ratio of 30,000 to 1 was appropriate for one important reason: large legislative bodies typically did not protect liberty, they destroyed it. "The people can never err more than in supposing that by multiplying their representatives beyond a certain limit, they strengthen the barrier against the government of a few. Experience will forever admonish them that, on the contrary, AFTER SECURING A SUFFICIENT NUMBER FOR THE PURPOSE OF SAFETY, OF LOCAL INFORMATION, AND OF DIFFUSIVE SYMPATHY WITH THE WHOLE SOCIETY, they will counteract their own views by every addition to their representatives. The countenance of the government may become more democratic, but the soul that animates it will be more oligarchic."[11]

Both Dana and Wilson claimed that the Constitution "sprang" from the States and, with its limited or "enumerated" powers, a small legislative body was sufficient to handle the *general* business of the United States. Had the Congress been charged with the minutiae of State legislative issues, both would have agreed that Congress was too small to handle the task. As Wilson said during the Pennsylvania Ratifying Convention, "To support, with vigor, a single government over the whole extent of the United States, would demand a system of the most unqualified and the most unremitted despotism."[12] Their arguments were persuasive enough on this and other issues to help swing a few teetering votes toward ratification, particularly in Massachusetts.

Perhaps, however, opponents of the Constitution were slightly more prophetic when they suggested that representation would ultimately be set at a ratio too large to adequately represent the people. The initial first amendment in the proposed Bill of Rights in 1789 would have solved this problem. "After the first enumeration required by the first article of the Constitution, there shall be one representative for every thirty thousand, until the number shall amount to one hundred, after which the proportion shall be so regulated by Congress, that there shall not be less than one hundred representatives, nor less than one representative for every forty thousand persons, until the number of representatives shall amount to two hundred, after which the proportion shall be so regulated by Congress, that there shall not be less than two hundred representatives, nor more than one representative for every fifty thousand."[13] If it had been adopted, the current House of Representatives would have around 6,000 members, too large to do business as Madison suggested in Federalist No. 58. But had the founding generation been able to foresee the current ratio (700,000 to 1 in 2011), they would have considered it an outlandish affront to the principle of self-government. The problem could be solved through decentralization or by adhering to the Constitution *as ratified*, where the general government handled the *general* business of the Union, not the specific concerns of every city, county, and political district in the United States, requiring, as Pennsylvanian James Wilson reminded us, "a system of the most unqualified and the most unremitted despotism."

The Senate

"The Senate of the United States shall be composed of two Senators from each State, chosen by the Legislature thereof, for six Years; and each Senator shall have one vote." **Original Article I, Section 3.**

Without the original construction of the Senate—with the legislatures of each State electing two senators, each with one vote—the Constitution would not have been ratified or even made it out of the Philadelphia Convention. The Framers designed the Senate to preserve the equality of the States; to maintain a measure of State control over the general government; and to be the "aristocratic" chamber to restrain the potential excesses of the "mob" in the House. Senators have to be older, thirty as opposed to twenty-five, and have a longer residence in the United States, nine as opposed to seven years. James Madison explained that the more stringent qualifications for the Upper House were necessitated by the weight of the office. "The propriety of these distinctions is explained by the nature of the senatorial trust," he argued, "which requiring greater extent of information and stability of character, requires at the same time that the senator should have reached a period of life most likely to supply these advantages.… The term of nine years appears to be a prudent mediocrity between a total exclusion of adopted citizens, whose merit and talents may claim a share in the public confidence; and an indiscriminate and hasty admission of them, which might create a channel for foreign influence on the national councils."[14]

Edmund Randolph stated that the Senate was "to provide a cure for the evils under which the United States labored; that, in tracing these evils to their origin, every man had found it in the turbulence and follies of democracy; that some check therefore was to be sought for against this tendency of our governments; and that a good Senate seemed most likely to answer the purpose." Pierce Butler spoke against proportioning the upper house on the basis of population (as the Virginia Plan had done) because that would "destroy all that balance and security of interests among the states which it was necessary to preserve." Roger Sherman thought each State should have one member in the Senate, a recommendation that laid the groundwork for the eventual compromise on the issue of proportional or State representation in the Upper House.[15]

In May 1787, in the early days of the Philadelphia Convention, Richard Dobbs Spaight of North Carolina had moved that State legislatures should choose the members of the Senate. The idea was proposed again in June 1787 when John Dickinson of Delaware argued "that the members of the second branch ought to be chosen by the individual legislatures." Sherman immediately seconded the motion, believing that this would maintain "a due harmony between the two governments...." Dickinson then explained his reasoning. He thought the "states would be better collected through their governments than immediately from the people at large; secondly, because he wished for the Senate to consist of the most distinguished characters...."[16] Later, Dickinson said, "The preservation of the states in a certain degree of agency is indispensible. It will produce that collision between the different authorities which should be wished for in order to check each other. To attempt to abolish the states altogether, would degrade the councils of our country, would be impracticable, would be ruinous." He continued, "If the state governments were excluded from all agency in the national one, and all power drawn from the people at large, the consequence would be, that the national government would move in the same direction as the state governments now do, and would run into all the same mischiefs. The reform would only unite the thirteen small streams into one great current, pursuing the same course without any opposition whatever."[17] Of course, Dickinson was referring to the problems several States were facing in 1787—such as, depreciated paper money, excessive democracy, and high taxes. Dickinson, then, saw the States as a hedge against the general government, a check on its power.

George Mason of Virginia agreed. "Whatever power may be necessary for the national government, a certain portion must necessarily be left with the states. It is impossible for one power to pervade the extreme parts of the United States, so as to carry equal justice to them. The state legislatures, also, ought to have some means of defending themselves against encroachments of the national government. In every other department, we have studiously endeavored to provide for its self-defense. Shall we leave the states alone unprovided with the means for this purpose?" He understood that there was "a danger on both sides…but we have only seen the evils arising on the side of the state governments. Those on the other side remain to be displayed."[18] Dickinson's motion passed 10 to 0. It can thus be said that the Framers considered the direct election of senators by the people as impolitic. Certainly, men such as James Wilson and other nationalists pushed for it, but the more moderate men from both large and small States disagreed and provided a way for the States to have a prominent role in the general government.

Madison explained in Federalist No. 62 that the design of the Senate was "probably the most congenial with the public opinion. It is recommended by the double advantage of favouring a select appointment, and of giving to the state governments such an agency in the formation of the federal government, as must secure the authority of the former; and may form a convenient link between the two systems." Furthermore, "In this spirit it may be remarked, that the equal vote allowed to each state, is at once a constitutional recognition of the portion of sovereignty remaining in the individual states, and an instrument for preserving that residuary sovereignty." Ultimately, Madison believed this would guard "against an improper consolidation of the states into one simple republic."[19]

The Senate acts as a check on all three branches of government. It can block legislation originating in the House of Representatives; it can block executive appointments to both the executive and judicial branches; it can block foreign treaties; and it has the "sole

Power to try all Impeachments." All the Founders understood the Senate to be the chamber where the States could check the authority of the general government.

Madison argued that the Senate offered a great advantage for the prevention of legislative tyranny, for "no law or resolution can now be passed without the concurrence first of a majority of the people, and then of a majority of the states."[20] Tench Coxe of Pennsylvania, writing as "A Freeman" in 1788, argued that the check on appointment powers was the surest safeguard for State interests. "*The Senate can reject them all*, and independently give their reasons to the people and the legislatures. That they will often do so, we cannot doubt, when we remember *where their private interests, affections and connexions lie*, to whom they will owe *their seats*—to whom they must look for *future favors* of the same kind."[21] He, of course, was referring to the States.

Yet, there was some alarm among the founding generation concerning the inability of the States to recall senators. In New York, Gilbert Livingston introduced a resolution during the State Ratifying Convention that would have allowed New York not only to recall a senator if necessary, but also to mandate a rotation in office. John Lansing of New York argued that because the Senate was to be the State hedge against the general government, recall was "the only thing which can give the states a control over the Senate."[22] George Mason followed a similar line at the Virginia Ratifying Convention. "They cannot be recalled," he said, "in all that time for misconduct, and at the end of that long term may again be elected. What will be the operation of this? Is it not probable, that those Gentlemen who will be elected Senators will fix themselves in the federal town, and become citizens of that town more than of our State? They will purchase a good seat in or near the town, and become inhabitants of that place.... The Senators living at that spot will vote themselves handsome pay, without incurring any additional expences."[23]

Proponents of the Constitution, such as Alexander Hamilton, explained that the permanency of the Senate gave it vigor and stability. Hamilton argued that the Senate "together with the President, are to manage all of our concerns with foreign nations; they must understand all their political systems. This knowledge is not soon acquired.... Is it desirable, then, that new and unqualified members should be continually thrown into that body?"[24] John Jay of New York concurred. "It was wise therefore in the convention to provide not only that the power of making treaties should be committed to able and honest men, but also that they should continue in place a sufficient time to become perfectly acquainted with our national concerns.... The duration prescribed is such as will give them an opportunity of extending their political informations and of rendering their accumulating experience more and more beneficial to their country."[25]

Both Hamilton and Jay were alluding to the fact that the Senate was designed to be the non-democratic restraint on the House. John Dickinson likened it to the House of Lords in England, and several others followed a similar line of reasoning. With such extensive checks on every level of government, the Senate, according to the Framers, required longer terms and more polished representatives. This is why Roger Sherman said he "opposed elections by the people, in districts, as not likely to produce such fit men as elections by state legislatures."[26]

Madison aptly summarized the overall defense of the Senate when he wrote in Federalist No. 63 that "liberty may be endangered by the abuses of liberty, as well as by the abuses of power...and that the former rather than the latter is apparently most to be apprehended by the United States." But "Before [the Senate can become a 'dangerous preeminence in the government' it] must in the first place corrupt itself; must next corrupt the state legislatures, must then corrupt the house of representatives, and must finally corrupt the people at large.... Is there any man who can seriously persuade himself, that the proposed senate can, by any possible means within the compass of human address, arrive at the object of lawless ambition, through all these obstructions?"[27] Of course, the Seventeenth Amendment to the Constitution (the direct election of senators) removed one barrier to possible corruption and ultimately changed the nature and design of the Senate. Most of the Founders would not have supported this and would argue for its repeal.

Elections

"The Times, Places, and Manner of holding Elections for Senators and Representatives, shall be prescribed in each State by the Legislature thereof, but the Congress may at any time by Law make or alter such Regulations, except as to the Places of Chusing Senators." **Article I, Section 4.**

To modern Americans, the wording of Article I, Section 4 probably seems innocuous. The federal government, it appears, should have the final say in how elections are organized for sending members to the United States Congress. But, this was not universally accepted in 1787 (when the Constitution was written) or during the State Ratifying Conventions when it was sold to the States. Like other provisions of the Constitution, Article I, Section 4 became a debate over State sovereignty versus central power.

On 6 August 1787, the Committee of Detail presented a revised draft of the Constitution to the general convention at Philadelphia. Article VI, Section 1 on the draft stated, "The times, and places, and manner, of holding the elections of the members of each House, shall be prescribed by the legislature of each state; but their provisions concerning them may, at any time, be altered by the legislature of the United States."[28] Charles Pinckney and John Rutledge of South Carolina moved to strike what amounted to a federal veto over State control of federal elections. "The states, they contended, could and must be relied on in such cases."[29] But they were in the minority.

Nathaniel Gorham of Massachusetts responded that Pinckney and Rutledge were wrong because their proposal would be similar to restraining "the British Parliament from regulating the circumstances of elections, leaving the business to the counties themselves." Madison was much more direct. He called this power a "necessity" because "state legislatures will sometimes fail or refuse to consult the common interest at the expense of their local convenience or prejudices."[30] And Gouverneur Morris chimerically responded that "the states might make false returns and then make no provisions for new elections."[31] Morris often reprimanded members of the Convention for making fantastical suppositions, but on this occasion he made one himself. Only Roger Sherman defended the honor of the State legislatures, though he, like

Gorham, Madison, and Morris, voted against Pinckney and Rutledge. After the final vote was taken, Madison remarked in his journal that the article "was meant to give the national legislature a power not only to alter the provisions of the states, but to make regulations, in case the states should fail or refuse altogether."[32]

Such a nationalistic outlook was bound to receive criticism. Writing as "The Federal Farmer," Richard Henry Lee of Virginia emphasized that "the branches of the legislature are essential parts of the fundamental compact, and ought to be so fixed by the people, that the legislature cannot alter itself by modifying the elections of its own members." He pointed out that Article I, Section 4 gave the Congress the power to do just that: to overrule the right of the people (exercised through their State legislatures), to determine how their representatives were elected to the central government.[33] Abraham Holmes of Massachusetts, writing anonymously as "Vox Populi" to the *Massachusetts Gazette* in October 1787, wondered if "Congress could possibly be in any measure as good judges of the time, place and manner of elections as the legislatures of the several respective states"[34] and said it was lunacy to suppose—as Article I, Section 4 seemed to imply—that State legislatures might fail to ensure their State's representation in Congress with proper elections.

Perhaps the most eloquent writer in opposition to the Constitution, "Brutus" of New York, argued that Article I, Section 4 would ultimately produce "such changes as entirely to alter a government, subvert a free constitution, and rivet the chains on a free people before they perceived they are forged. Had the power of regulating elections been left under the direction of the state legislatures, where the people are not only nominally but substantially represented, it would have been secure...."[35] Luther Martin of Maryland cited Article I, Section 4 as the surest evidence that the Framers intended to consolidate the States. He called it "a provision...*designed* for the *utter extinction* and *abolition of all State governments*."[36]

The Ratifying Conventions in Virginia, Massachusetts, New York, and Pennsylvania all debated the Framers' intent regarding Article I, Section 4. In Massachusetts, Charles Turner objected to the language of the section, stating it would "give to Congress a power that they can abuse." He later called it "a genuine power for Congress to perpetuate themselves—a power that cannot be unexceptionably exercised in any case whatever."[37] Patrick Henry lamented that with this power, "the elections may be held at one place, and the most inconvenient in the state; or they may be at remote distances from those who have a right of suffrage: hence nine out of ten must either not vote at all, or vote for strangers; for the most influential characters will be applied to, to know who are the most proper to be chosen. I repeat, that the control of Congress over the *manner*, &c., of electing, well warrants this idea. The natural consequence will be, that this democratic branch will possess none of the public confidence; the people will be prejudiced against representatives chosen in such an injudicious manner."[38] Samuel Jones of New York "apprehended that the clause might be so construed as to deprive the states of an essential right, which, in the true design of the Constitution, was to be reserved to them."[39] And Samuel Spencer of North Carolina argued that the section "apparently looks forward to a consolidation of the government of the United States, when the state legislatures may entirely decay away."[40]

With these objections in mind, proponents had to justify the inclusion of the federal check on State control of elections. Madison's remark that this power was designed to enhance the power of the general government was unknown to the public or to the Ratifying Conventions, and had it been, there might have been a more substantial attempt to alter the language. James Wilson essentially created the "talking points" for proponents on the subject when he argued in October 1787 that, "The members of the Senate are elected by the state legislatures. If those legislatures possessed, uncontrolled, the power of prescribing the times, places, and manner, of electing members of the House of Representatives, the members of one branch of the general legislature would be the tenants at will of the electors of the other branch; and the general government would lie prostrate at the mercy of the legislatures of the several states."[41]

Hamilton spilled considerable ink on the subject in the Federalist essays. In Federalist No. 59, he simply stated that Article I, Section 4 was an outgrowth of the "plain proposition, that *every government ought to contain in itself the means of its own preservation.*" More specifically, Hamilton relayed the fears of the members of the Philadelphia Convention when he stated in the same essay that, "Nothing can be more evident, than that an exclusive power of regulating elections for the National Government, in the hands of the State Legislatures, would leave the existence of the Union entirely at their mercy. They could at any moment annihilate it, by neglecting to provide for the choice of persons to administer its affairs."[42]

Proponents in other States followed a similar line of thinking, and most cited the refusal of Rhode Island to send delegates to the Congress under the Articles of Confederation. Rufus King of Massachusetts thought that, should "no power be vested in Congress to revise their Laws, or to provide other Regulations, the Union might be dismembered and dissolved without a constitutional power to prevent it."[43] Fisher Ames of Massachusetts preferred the "general government" having this power "than a foreign state," such as "Rhode Island and Georgia."[44]

James Iredell of North Carolina, a proponent of the Constitution and later Supreme Court Justice, sought to soothe fears over the provision by offering an amendment to the Constitution that would have forbidden the Congress from interfering in elections unless "the legislature of any state shall neglect, refuse, or be disabled by invasion or rebellion, to prescribe the same."[45] Aedanus Burke of South Carolina proposed a similar amendment in the First Congress but was defeated by five votes. During debate over that amendment, Roger Sherman, Madison, and Fisher Ames voiced their unqualified support for Article I, Section 4 as written, with Sherman going so far as to say that altering it would "subvert the Government."[46]

Governor Samuel Johnston of North Carolina rightly pointed out during the First State Ratifying Convention that the language of Article I, Section 4 was "altogether useless, because they [the States] can put an end to the general government by refusing to choose senators," because senatorial elections, conducted by the State legislatures, were not covered by Article I, Section 4. William Richardson Davie, perhaps the most respected man in North Carolina, emphasized that "the states, sir, can put a final period to the government.... If the state legislatures think proper, they may refuse to choose senators, and the government must be destroyed."[47] Even Hamilton conceded, "It is certainly true, that the State Legislatures, by forbearing the appointment of Senators, may destroy the National Government."[48] This was another check by the States on the power of the central government that was eradicated by the Seventeenth Amendment to the Constitution.

Compensation

"The Senators and Representatives shall receive a Compensation for their Services, to be ascertained by Law, and paid out of the Treasury of the United States...."
Article I, Section 6, Clause 1.

With 2010 congressional salaries ranging from $174,000 to $233,000 a year, and with the additional perquisites associated with the job ranging in the millions in some cases, the issue of congressional compensation has received some attention by concerned American citizens. And though not as controversial as other provisions in the Constitution, this issue was the subject of considerable debate during the Philadelphia Convention.

The first draft of the Constitution allowed for a "liberal compensation for members" of Congress to be paid by the State legislatures. Madison thought the salaries should be fixed and argued against the States having a role in the process. Leaving the language alone would "create an improper dependence [on the States]; *and to leave them to regulate their own wages was an indecent thing, and might in time prove a dangerous one*" (emphasis added). George Mason observed that should the States be allowed to set the compensation, they "might reduce the provision so low, that, as had already happened in choosing delegates to Congress [under the Articles of Confederation], the question would be, not who were most fit to be chosen, but who were most willing to serve." Benjamin Franklin proposed substituting "liberal" with "moderate" but urged a fixed compensation. He thought history had proven that "abuses...once begun" were difficult to arrest. The language of the clause was changed to allow for funds to be drafted from the "national treasury" for compensation.[49]

There were members of the Philadelphia Convention, however, who favored State control over congressional compensation. Oliver Ellsworth of Connecticut and Hugh Williamson of North Carolina argued that because of the differences in the customs, manners, and habits of the several States, it would "impede the system" to have representatives paid by the "national treasury." Williamson further suggested that the "poor" members of any new Western States would be a drag on the established States in the East. "He did not think ... that the [Eastern States] ought to pay the expense of men who would be employed in thwarting their measures and interests." Ellsworth explained, "If we are jealous of the state governments, they will be so of us. If, on going home [after the Philadelphia Convention], I tell them we gave the general government such powers because we could not trust you, will they adopt it [the Constitution]? And without their approbation it is a nullity."

State control over salaries was narrowly defeated,[50] But when the Committee of Detail presented another draft of the Constitution in August 1787, the States again had control over congressional salaries. Ellsworth had since changed his mind and advocated altering the language to read "that they should be paid out of the treasury of the United States...." Only Luther Martin and Pierce Butler advocated giving the States the power over salaries: Butler because he feared that senators would "lose sight of their constituents, unless dependent on them for their support," and Martin because he thought the Senate, as the representative body of the States, "ought to be paid by the States." Ellsworth's proposal passed nine to two with the general consensus being that this would provide some level of independence for the Congress.[51]

Still, the majority, at least initially, opposed giving Congress the power to establish pay for its members. When James Wilson moved in June 1787 that the "national legislature" should have the power to set its own salaries, the proposal was defeated seven to two. After some deliberation, the phrase "adequate compensation" was substituted for the word "fixed," though adequate was not properly defined. Both Benjamin Franklin and Charles Cotesworth Pinckney of South Carolina argued that senators should not receive a salary. When the debate over the issue resumed in August, Ellsworth attempted to fix the salary. As he had earlier in the Convention, Madison agreed that salaries should be fixed, but offered no set sum. Gouverneur Morris thought there "was no reason to fear that they would overpay themselves," but he was in the minority.

Roger Sherman spoke, as he often did during the Convention, as the voice of reason and moderation. He thought "the best plan would be, to fix a moderate allowance, to be paid out of the national treasury, and let the states make such additions as they might judge fit." Sherman recommended five dollars a day. But the Convention could decide neither on a set salary nor on whether compensation should be the same for representatives and senators.[52] The Convention eventually decided to leave it to the discretion of the Congress "to be ascertained by law." It was a weak solution not lost during the ratification debates.

In December 1787, an essay written by "Cornelius" in the *Hampshire Chronicle* argued that the intent of this Article was to "not only enhance the expense of the federal government to a degree that will be truly burdensome; but also, to increase the luxury and extravagance, in general, which threatens the ruin of the United States...."[53] Nathaniel Barrell of Massachusetts stated he opposed the Constitution in part because Congress may "fix their own salaries without allowing any controul."[54] Timothy Winn of Massachusetts was shocked that any man would be willing to "put the whole of their property into the hands of any set of men...for the term of six years, and to give them authority to appoint their own officers and commissioners, to state their own salaries, and to point out to their constituents the method in which they shall pay them, and to enforce their orders by an army."[55] Even Rufus King, a friend of the Constitution, thought that arguments against unchecked compensation had weight.[56]

In the Virginia Ratifying Convention, Patrick Henry prophetically warned against the open-ended nature of Article I, Section 6, Clause 1.

> The pay of the Members is, by the Constitution, to be fixed by themselves, without limitation or restraint. They may therefore indulge themselves in the fullest extent. They may make their compensations as high as they please. I suppose, if they be good men, their own delicacy will lead them to be satisfied with moderate salaries. But there is no security in this, should they be otherwise inclined. I really believe that if the State Legislatures were to fix their pay, no inconvenience would result from it, and the public mind would be better satisfied.[57]

When the first Congress convened in 1789, salaries were set at $5 per diem, the sum originally supported by most of the members of the Philadelphia Convention. That would equate to roughly $125 per day in 2010 dollars. Even if congressmen claimed to be working every day of the week (earning them $46, 625), their salaries would be lower by more than $100,000 from current pay rates. It was not until 1855 that members of Congress began receiving an annual salary of $3,000—about $76,000 in 2010 dollars, or less than half of what congressmen make today.

It wasn't until the Twenty-seventh Amendment to the Constitution, ratified in 1992, that a modest electoral check was put on Congress's power to raise its own salaries. ("No law, varying the compensation of the Senators and Representatives, shall take effect, until an election of Representatives shall have intervened.") Even that met stiff legal challenges from incumbent congressmen who balked at a restriction on their unbridled ability to continually increase their own salaries.

Patrick Henry and other members of the founding generation worried about the probability of congressional excesses—what Madison called indecency—and were they alive to see how lavishly congressmen reward themselves today, they would surely be appalled. Across the board, the Founding Fathers viewed service in the government as a duty rather than a station. That, more than anything else, is what separates the founding generation from the political class today.

Congressional Powers

Article I, Sections 7, 8, and 9, are the most important pieces of the Constitution, and not coincidentally received the most scrutiny. They provide Congress with the power of the "Sword and the Purse" and contain most of the "vague" clauses of the Constitution—such as the "General Welfare Clause," the "Necessary and Proper Clause," the "Commerce Clause," and the "Post Roads Clause"—that have been used to expand the power of the general government. "Vague," however, is a relative term. In the

State ratifying debates, each "vague" clause was explained in terms of the limits of congressional power.

The Power of the Purse

"All Bills for raising Revenue shall originate in the House of Representatives; but the Senate may propose or concur with Amendments as on other Bills."

When the Committee of Detail presented a draft of the Constitution on 6 August 1787, it contained the following section: "All bills for raising or appropriating money, and for fixing the salaries of the officers of government, shall originate in the House of Representatives, and shall not be altered or amended by the Senate."[58] Charles Pinckney of South Carolina moved to strike the entire section, and argued that, "If the Senate can be trusted with the many great powers proposed, it surely may be trusted with that of originating money bills." Most supported Pinckney, but George Mason gave a compelling argument for leaving the language alone. First, "to strike out the section was to unhinge the compromise of which it made a part." Second, because the Senate, in his mind, was an "aristocratic body, like the screw in mechanics working its way by slow degrees, and holding fast whatever it gains," it should never be accused of encroaching on the power of the people, nor should "the purse-strings…be put into its hands." Nathaniel Gorham offered a simple solution: the Senate should be allowed to amend but not originate money bills.[59] Pinckney's motion passed and the matter would be addressed later in the Convention, but it was clear that the Framers believed the power of the purse should be left in the hands of the "people."

When the Convention again broached the issue, John Dickinson made one of the more important speeches of the summer. He emphasized that "experience must be our only guide. Reason may mislead us. It was not reason that discovered the singular and admirable mechanism of the English constitution. It was not reason that discovered or ever could have discovered, the odd . . . the absurd mode of trial by jury. Accidents probably produced these discoveries, and experience has given a sanction to them. This is, then, our guide." Hence, because "eight states have inserted in their constitutions the exclusive right of originating money bills in favor of the popular branch of the legislature," and because, "most of them . . . allowed the other branch to amend. . . . This . . . would be proper for us to do."[60]

The beauty of Dickinson's address relates to his admission that the Constitution should not be the best document the delegates to the Convention could imagine, but should rely on time-tested maxims of government, society, and law. Others had suggested that "experience" should guide their actions, but Dickinson said it best. They were not reinventing the government of the United States— the rejection of Madison's Virginia Plan drove that home—they were creating a general government the people of the States would accept, which argued in favor of relying on customary and familiar government powers. As Edmund Randolph said after Dickinson finished, "[My] principle object . . . was to prevent popular objections against the plan, and to secure its passage."[61] Dickinson's suggestion served as the basis of Article I, Section 7, Clause 1.

There was little debate on the language of Article I, Section 7, Clause 1 in the State ratifying conventions. Theophilus Parsons of Massachusetts defended the clause by pointing out that if the Senate could not propose amendments, it became in essence a hostage of the

House.[62] William Grayson of Virginia, an opponent of the Constitution, objected to the clause, insisting that, "The Senate could strike out every word of a bill, except the word *whereas,* or any other introductory word, and might substitute new words of their own. As the state of Delaware was not as large as the county of Augusta, and Rhode Island was still less, and yet had an equal suffrage in the Senate, he could not see the propriety of giving them this power, but referred it to the judgment of the house." Madison attempted to appease Grayson by emphasizing that as "senators are appointed by the states… they will guard the political interests of the states…in their amendments to money bills. I think this power, for these considerations, is useful and necessary."[63] Grayson remained opposed, but because a majority of the States already had this provision in their constitutions, Grayson had few supporters. Dickinson was proven right that experience and custom were the best guides to drafting the Constitution.

The General Welfare

"The Congress shall have Power To lay and collect Taxes, Duties, Imposts and Excises, to pay the Debts and provide for the common Defense and general Welfare of the United States; but all Duties, Imposts, and Excises shall be uniform throughout the United States."

Save the "Necessary and Proper Clause," and the "Supremacy Clause" of Article 6, no other clause has been misinterpreted or misquoted as much as the "General Welfare Clause" contained in Article I, Section 8, Clause 1. For example, in March 2010, Representative John Conyers of Michigan declared that because of the "good and welfare clause" of the Constitution, President Barack Obama's healthcare legislation was constitutional. He continued, "All the constitutional scholars that I know, I'm Chairman of Judiciary Committee as you know, they all say that there's nothing unconstitutional in this bill, and if there were I would have tried to correct it...." It seems that ignorance of the Constitution extends beyond Congress to Conyers' friends who are "constitutional scholars."

The fact is, the "General Welfare Clause" was in no way designed to deal with legislation like Obamacare. Very little was said about the "General Welfare Clause" in the ratification debates because its meaning was obvious to the Framers. The "General Welfare Clause" of the Constitution was lifted from Article 3 of the Articles of Confederation, which read: "The said states hereby severally enter into a firm league of friendship with each other for the common defense, the security of their liberties and their mutual and general welfare; binding themselves to assist each other against all force offered to, or attacks made upon them, or any of them, on account of religion, sovereignty, trade, or any other pretence whatever." In the Virginia Plan, Madison resolved that "the Articles of Confederation ought to be so corrected and enlarged as to accomplish the objects proposed by their institution; namely, 'common defense, security of liberty, and general welfare.'"[64] It was clear to those who signed the Articles and served in the first Congresses of the United States that the "general welfare" meant legislation that benefited each State and defended the liberties, "religion, sovereignty, [and] trade," of the several States. The Constitution gave the new Congress the power to raise revenue for such purposes, but it did not alter the original meaning of the "general welfare."

The initial language of Article I, Section 8, Clause 1, read: "The Legislature *shall* fulfill the engagements and discharge the debts of the U. S, & shall have the power to lay & collect taxes duties imposts & excises." It wasn't until late in the Philadelphia Convention that a recommendation was made to add the phrase "common defense and general welfare" to the clause, and that was initially rejected because the Convention thought it was "unnecessary." In essence, every delegate knew that the term "general welfare" was redundant because the enumerated list of powers clearly was intended for both the common defense and general welfare of the Union. Roger Sherman made the motion to add the phrase, but it did not appear on a draft of the Constitution until September.[65]

Because it was Sherman who essentially added the phrase to the Constitution, it would be appropriate to determine how he defined the "general welfare." In June 1787, he said, "The objects of the Union...were few—first, defence against foreign danger; second, against internal disputes and a resort to force; thirdly, treaties with foreign nations; fourthly, regulating foreign commerce, and drawing revenue from it.... All other matters, civil and criminal, would be much better in the hands of the states."[66] That was the "general welfare and common defense." David Ramsey of South Carolina similarly explained that the powers of Congress are "confined to provide for the *common defense and general welfare* of the United States. If they apply money to any other purposes, they exceed their powers.... It would be tedious to go over all the powers of Congress, but it would be easy to shew that they all may be referred to this single principle, 'that the general concerns of the *union* [not individuals] ought to be managed by the general government'"[67] (emphasis added).

Not everyone, however, agreed that the general government would abide by such a limited definition of the "general welfare." "Timoleon" of New York opined in 1787 that "the *general welfare* is as unlimited as actions and things are that may disturb or benefit that general welfare. A right being given to *tax* for the general welfare, necessarily includes the right of judging what is for the general welfare, and a right of judging what is for the general welfare, as *necessarily* includes a power of protecting, defending, and promoting it by all such means as are fitted to that end."[68] "Brutus" summarized the argument: "To provide for the general welfare, is an abstract proposition, which mankind differ in the explanation of, as much as they do on any political or moral proposition that can be proposed."[69] William Symmes Jr. correctly argued that the "term 'general welfare' might be applied to any expenditure whatever."[70] "A Federal Republican" echoed this position and for that reason thought that "their power should have been accurately defined."[71]

Madison spoke of the "General Welfare Clause" a number of times in detail both before and after the Constitution was ratified, and, because he wrote the Virginia Plan and was the first to lift the phrase from the Articles of Confederation, his opinion has merit. In Federalist No. 41 Madison questioned why anyone would have a problem with the phrase "general welfare." "But what colour can the objection have, when a specification of the objects alluded to by these general terms, immediately follows; and is not even separated by a longer pause than a semicolon…. Nothing is more natural or common than first to use a general phrase, and then to explain and qualify it by a recital of particulars."[72] And while on the floor of Congress in 1791, he said the general welfare "was limited to acts laying taxes for them; and the general purposes themselves were limited and explained by the particular enumeration subjoined. To understand these terms in any sense, that would justify the power in question, would give to Congress an unlimited power; would render nugatory the enumeration of particular powers; would supercede all the powers reserved to the state governments. These terms are copied from the articles of confederation; had it ever been pretended, that they were to be understood otherwise than as here explained?"[73] Hamilton may have said it best when he suggested that the "leading objects of the federal government...are to maintain domestic peace, and provide for the common defense." "Domestic peace" equaled "general welfare."[74]

Taxes

The general opposition to the "General Welfare Clause" stemmed not from the clause itself but from the unlimited potential of congressional taxing power for the "general welfare." It was assumed by most opponents that Congress would abuse its authority to "lay and collect Taxes," and would ultimately suffocate the States' ability to do the same. Elbridge Gerry of Massachusetts fired a warning shot against congressional taxing power when he argued in August 1787 that "the legislature could not be trusted with such a power. It might ruin the country. It might be exercised partially, raising one and depressing another part of it."[75]

Richard Henry Lee, as the "Federal Farmer," wrote in 1787 that "to lay and collect internal taxes, in this extensive country, must require a great number of congressional ordinances, immediately operating upon the body of the people; these must continually interfere with the state laws, and thereby produce disorder and general dissatisfaction, till the one system of laws or the other, operating upon the same subjects, shall be abolished.... Further, as to internal taxes, the state governments will have concurrent powers with the general government, and both may tax the same objects in the same year; and the objection that the general government may suspend a state tax, as a necessary measure for the promoting the collection of a federal tax, is not without foundation."[76]

"Brutus" wrote the most extensive and detailed opposition to congressional taxing power in Essay No. 5:

> To detail the particulars comprehended in the general terms, taxes, duties, imposts and excises, would require a volume, instead of a single piece in a news-paper. Indeed it would be a task far beyond my ability, and to which no one can be competent, unless possessed of a mind capable of comprehending every possible source of revenue; for they extend to every possible way of raising money, whether by direct or indirect taxation. Under this clause may be imposed a poll-tax, a land-tax, a tax on houses and buildings, on windows and fire places, on cattle and on all kinds of personal property:—It extends to duties on all kinds of goods to any amount, to tonnage and poundage on vessels, to duties on written instruments, newspapers, almanacks, and books:—It comprehends an excise on all kinds of liquors, spirits, wines, cyder, beer, etc. and indeed takes in duty or excise on every necessary or conveniency of life; whether of foreign or home growth or manufactory. In short, we can have no conception of any way in which a government can raise money from the people, but what is included in one or other of [these] general terms. We may say then that this clause commits to the hands of the general legislature every conceivable source of revenue within the United States. Not only are these terms very comprehensive, and extend to a

vast number of objects, but the power to lay and collect
has great latitude; it will lead to the passing a vast number of laws, which may affect the personal rights of the
citizens of the states, expose their property to fines and
confiscation, and put their lives in jeopardy: it opens a
door to the appointment of a swarm of revenue and
excise officers to prey upon the honest and industrious
part of the community, eat up their substance, and riot
on the spoils of the country.[77]

Or, as he put it in Essay No. 6: "To all these different classes of
people, and in all these circumstances, in which it will attend them,
the language in which it will address them, will be GIVE! GIVE!"[78]

Congress's taxing authority was a hot issue during the State
ratifying conventions. Samuel Spencer of North Carolina called the
taxing power "too extensive, as it embraces all possible powers of
taxation, and gives up to Congress every possible article of taxation
that can ever happen."[79] Abraham White of Massachusetts said, "In
giving this power, we give up every thing; and Congress, with the
purse-strings in their hands, will use the sword with a witness."[80]
William Bodman of Massachusetts called it "dangerous" and
questioned "whether it was necessary to give Congress power to do
harm, in order to enable them to do good. It had been said, that the
sovereignty of the states remains with them; but if Congress has the
power to lay taxes, and, in cases of negligence or non-compliance,
can send a power to collect them, he thought that the idea of
sovereignty was destroyed."[81] Samuel Thompson of Massachusetts
had the most poignant question of the group: "It has been said that
there was no such danger here. I will suppose they were to attempt
the experiment, after we have given them all our money, established

them in a federal town, given them the power of coining money and raising a standing *army*, and to establish their arbitrary government; what resources have the people left?"[82]

Proponents of congressional taxing power built a strong defense on a unanimous theme: this power was necessary to defend the Union and stabilize the government. James Wilson refuted the vivid and horrid description of tax collectors offered by "Brutus" and others when he said in the Pennsylvania Ratifying Convention that, "It has been common with the gentlemen, on this subject, to present us with frightful pictures. We are told of the hosts of tax-gatherers that will swarm through the land; and whenever taxes are mentioned, military force seems to be an attending idea. I think I may venture to predict that the taxes of the general government, if any shall be laid, will be more equitable, and much less expensive, than those imposed by state governments."[83] Oliver Ellsworth argued that such a power was necessary in the case of war, and said, "A government which can command but half its resources is like a man with but one arm to defend himself."[84] Richard Dobbs Spaight contended, "It was absolutely necessary for the support of the general government to give it power to raise taxes. Government cannot exist without certain and adequate funds. Requisitions cannot be depended upon."[85]

Madison plainly spoke for the proponents of the document when he maintained during the Virginia Ratifying Convention that "a government which relies on thirteen independent sovereignties for the means of its existence, is a solecism in theory and a mere nullity in practice. Is it consistent with reason that such a government can promote the happiness of any people? It is subversive of every principle of sound policy, to trust the safety of a community with a government totally destitute of the means of protecting itself or its members."

Defense, stability, and liberty; that is what the founding generation considered the "general welfare," and the ability of the central authority to collect taxes was seen as essential for the preservation of those rights. Opponents were correct that Congress would eventually use the taxing power to "lay and collect Taxes" on virtually every item it could. Additionally, their prediction that the "General Welfare Clause" was too "abstract" has been proven accurate. But this should not be considered a badge of honor; in fact, quite the opposite. The founding generation viewed high taxes and expansive government as a curse rather than a blessing, and the proponents of the Constitution constantly sought to soothe the fears of the public by arguing that taxes would not be too high or the powers of government too broad.

One famous opponent of the Constitution, "An Old Whig," aptly summarized the opposition to the "general welfare" and congressional taxing power in 1787. "I am firmly persuaded that scarcely a man of common sense can be found, that does not wish for an efficient federal government, and lament that it has been delayed so long. Yet at the same time it is a matter of immense consequence, in establishing a government which is to last for ages, and which, if it be suffered to depart from the principles of liberty in the beginning, will in all probability, never return to them, that we consider carefully what sort of government we are about to form. Power is very easily increased; indeed it naturally grows in every government; but it hardly ever lessens."[86]

Credit, Commerce, and Coin

"To borrow money on the credit of the United States;
"To regulate Commerce with foreign Nations, and among the several States, and with the Indian Tribes;...

> "To coin Money, regulate the value thereof, and of
> foreign Coin, and fix the Standard of Weights and Mea-
> sures." **Article I, Section 8, Clauses 2, 3, and 5.**

Along with the power to tax, congressional power over commerce
also included the power to borrow and coin money. Combined,
these were intended to promote the "general welfare" by quelling
what Roger Sherman called "internal disputes" and by regulating
"foreign commerce." The so-called "Commerce Clause" has been
used to defend virtually every federal regulation of commerce since
John Marshall's famous opinion in *Gibbons v. Ogden* (1824), the
landmark case that established Congress's right to regulate interstate commerce.

The power to borrow money originally contained the line "to
emit bills on the credit of the United States." This equated to a
congressional power to print paper money. Gouverneur Morris
moved to strike that power, and he was hurriedly joined by several
members of the Convention from both the North and South.
Oliver Ellsworth called it "a favorable moment to shut and bar the
door against paper money.... Paper money can in no case be necessary. Give the government credit, and other resources will offer."
James Wilson said that barring paper money would have "the most
salutary influence on the credit of the United States," and Pierce
Butler "remarked that paper was a legal tender in no country in
Europe." George Read of Delaware was the most dramatic. He said,
"The words, if not struck out, would be as alarming as the mark of
the beast in Revelation."[87]

There were those who cautioned that removing this power
from the government could result in future calamity. Madison
thought it was more reasonable to prohibit paper money from
being common currency, but that "emergencies" may require

"promissory notes, in that shape." George Mason said he had a "mortal hatred for paper money, yet as he could not foresee all emergencies, he was unwilling to tie the hands of the legislature." Edmund Randolph echoed both Madison and Mason, though the vote to strike passed nine to two.[88] Luther Martin sarcastically criticized the decision in *Genuine Information No. VI*: "Sir, a majority of the convention, being wise beyond every event, and being willing to risque any political evil rather than admit the *idea* of a paper emission, in any *possible* case, refused to *trust* this authority to a government, to which they were *lavishing* the most *unlimited* powers of *taxation,* and to the *mercy* of which they were willing *blindly* to *trust* the *liberty* and *property* of the *citizens* of *every State* in the union; and they *erased* that clause from the system."[89]

The general disdain for paper money illustrated that most of the Framers intended to temper the excessive debt and struggling finances of the general government under the Articles of Confederation. Hence, the power to "coin money" naturally meant that only metals would be used as legal tender in the United States, particularly when coupled with a prohibition on State paper money in Article I, Section 10, Clause 1. Everyone understood that to be the case. Henry Knox of Massachusetts wrote in 1787 that the "proposed constitution affects deeply the projects of the paper money, and convenient politicians, it will set in motion every subelty [*sic*] and art they possess to retard its progress and frustrate its adoption."[90] One New Jersey commentator called paper money "that great instrument of fraud."[91] Writing as "A Landholder" in November 1787, Oliver Ellsworth reasoned that the prohibition on paper money would give "a new spring to business."[92] Edmund Pendleton of Virginia said in 1787, "The restrictions on Paper emissions & unjust tender Laws are alone of value Sufficient to outweigh all Objections to the System...."[93] Most historians suggest that both the Framers and Ratifiers understood the phrase "to coin Money" included the power to print paper, but judging from the historical record and the statements made during the Philadelphia Convention, the State ratifying conventions, and in the press, no such power was contemplated.

Because Congress, according to the Constitution, could not print worthless paper and had to rely on hard money, this naturally led to the issue of debt. How could the government retire the debt? How much debt was too much? Writing as "Cincinnatus," Arthur Lee of Virginia worried that the Constitution's prohibition of paper money would "grind the poor to dust." The debt, which he argued had been "swelled to its enormous size, by…enormous impositions," would be impossible to retire under the Constitution. "The new government, by promising too much, will involve itself in a disreputable breech of faith…."[94] "A Federal Republican" argued that the powers of Congress would lead to one thing: "many needless expenses" or, in other words, debt.[95]

"Brutus" had the best exposition on the subject during the months leading to ratification. "Under this authority [to borrow money], the Congress may mortgage any or all the revenues of the union, as a fund to loan money upon, and it is probably, in this way, they may borrow of foreign nations, a principal sum, the interest of which will be equal to the annual revenues of the country.—By this means, they may create a national debt, so large, as to exceed the ability of the country ever to sink. I can scarcely contemplate a greater calamity that could befal [sic] this country, than to be loaded with a debt exceeding their ability ever to discharge." He suggested that the power to borrow could be necessary in emergencies, "But it certainly ought never to be exercised, but on the most urgent occasions, and then we should not borrow of foreigners if we could possibly avoid it." He then recommended that such a power should have been "so restricted" as to make "it very difficult for the government to practise it. The present confederation requires the assent of nine states to exercise this, and a number of the other important powers of the confederacy—and it would certainly have been a wise provision in this constitution, to have made it necessary that two thirds of the members should assent to borrowing money—when the necessity was indispensible, this assent would always be given, and in no other cause ought it to be." Most important, "a power to borrow at discretion, without any limitation or restriction" was "unwise and improvident."[96]

Alexander Hamilton believed that retiring the debt should be a priority of the new government and wrote in Federalist No. 15 that without the Constitution, the United States had no "proper or satisfactory provision for [its] discharge."[97] David Ramsey of South Carolina contended that if the United States were dissolved, the South would be the "loser" because of the large amount of money it owed to foreign creditors.[98] Ratifying the Constitution, then, was necessary for self-preservation. But acquiring more debt, as the Constitution allowed Congress to do, particularly to foreign governments, threatened the sovereignty and stability of the Union. Even proponents of the Constitution admitted as much. Those who advocated paper money argued it made retiring the debt easier, but the objective of both proponents and opponents of the Constitution was the same: retire the debt. They would be shocked by the crippling amount owed by the United States today, and would undoubtedly argue for retiring the debt as quickly as possible, as well as dramatically shrinking the size of the government that acquired such debt.

The founding generation believed paper money and excessive debt were a double-barreled assault on the financial liberty and security of the public. But what did the founding generation think about commerce? The current central government uses the "Commerce Clause" as a tool to "regulate" foreign and domestic trade with restrictions on free enterprise. The founding generation, however, generally viewed the "Commerce Clause" as a way to *reduce* government restrictions that inhibited free commerce. In contrast to the current definition of the "Commerce Clause," the founding generation did not think Congress had the power to regulate *intrastate* commerce, only commerce "among the several States." As Edmund Pendleton said, "Trade & manufacturers should both be Free...."[99]

Late in his life, in his draft for a "Preface to Debates in the Convention of 1787," James Madison wrote a thorough discussion of why the Framers wrote the "Commerce Clause." Madison said, "The want of authy. in Congs. to regulate Commerce had produced in Foreign nations particularly G. B. a monopolizing policy injurious to the trade of the U. S. and destructive to their navigation...." Thus, foreign trade was the primary objective of the clause. Secondary was the effect such lack of authority had on the States. "The same want of a general power over Commerce led to an exercise of this power separately, by the States, wch not only proved abortive, but engendered rival, conflicting and angry regulations.... In sundry instances...the navigation laws treated the Citizens of other States as aliens."[100] Madison also referred to this power in Federalist No. 42 as that of a "superintending authority over the reciprocal trade of confederated States."[101]

Alexander Hamilton also presented it that way in Federalist No. 11. "An *unrestrained* intercourse between the States themselves will advance the trade of each, by an interchange of their respective productions, not only for the supply of reciprocal wants at home, but for *exportation to foreign markets*"[102] (emphasis added). Hamilton argued that without a general regulation of foreign commerce, States were competing against each other for foreign markets, often to their own detriment. Hamilton, in fact, defined "commerce" as "the whole system of foreign intercourse" and said that this was one of the "leading objects of the federal government, in which revenue is concerned."[103]

Everyone knew that "revenue" and "commerce" were joined at the hip. According to the Constitution, a mere majority is required to pass commercial legislation, in particular tariffs, or what were called "navigation laws." For most of the Philadelphia Convention, delegates from the Southern States insisted on a two-thirds majority to pass such legislation, because they did not want the "Commerce Clause" to be a Northern tool for regulating the South into economic ruin. Oliver Ellsworth of Connecticut sympathized with Southern fears and thought that changing the "middle and moderate ground" of a two-thirds majority would destroy the Union, "and not without bloodshed."[104]

On 29 August 1787, Charles Pinckney of South Carolina moved "that no act of the legislature for the purpose of regulating the commerce of the United States with foreign powers, among the several states, shall be passed without the assent of two thirds of the members of each House." He reasoned that because there were five distinct economic interests in the United States, this was necessary to prevent "oppressive regulations, if no check to a bare majority should be provided."

George Clymer of Pennsylvania was equally opposed to trade restrictions but argued for congressional regulation of foreign commerce as a foreign policy necessity: "The Northern and Middle States will be ruined, if not enabled to defend themselves against foreign regulations."[105] Clymer's view became the majority view, because he won over Southerners like Pierce Butler and John Rutledge of South Carolina, who accepted the requirement for a simple majority as a good faith effort to forge a Union that benefited and burdened all equally. Butler did not trust the North, and called the Northern and Southern interests "as different as the interests as Russia and Turkey," but in the spirit of "conciliating the affections of the Eastern States" he voted against a two-thirds majority. Rutledge trusted that the Northern States would not abuse the power to regulate trade, and thought that his Southern colleagues should take a "permanent view of the subject." Hugh Williamson and Richard Dobbs Spaight of North Carolina suggested that if the North became obnoxious, Southerners could simply build their own ships.[106] Still, it remained a matter of contention. During the Virginia Ratifying Convention, George Mason reminded the delegates that at the Philadelphia Convention, "eight states out of twelve...voted for requiring two thirds of the members present in each house to pass commercial and navigation laws."[107]

Whatever their differences over a majority or two-thirds vote, what is clear is that the founding generation thought of the "Commerce Clause" largely in terms of foreign trade, and saw it as regulating interstate commerce only in the sense of preventing States from erecting barriers to trade. They certainly did not anticipate that all economic activity would fall under the "Commerce Clause" and that the general government would seize the power to regulate *intrastate* as well as *interstate* commerce. John Marshall, who later ruled that Congress had such power, had served in the Virginia

Ratifying Convention in 1788. But if his position had held the day then, the Constitution would not have been ratified.

Several States proposed amendments to Article I, Section 8, to prohibit the federal government from creating monopolies or corporations. These proposed amendments can be found in Appendix B.

Post Roads and Internal Improvements

"To establish Post Offices and post Roads." **Article I, Section 8, Clause 7.**

The power to build roads, canals, railroads, bridges, and even lighthouses or other "internal improvements" is an implied power not specifically enumerated in the Constitution. It has been often exercised, however, from the early federal period to the present. Generally, proponents will cite either the "General Welfare Clause," the "Necessary and Proper Clause," the "Commerce Clause," or the "Post Roads Clause" of Article I, Section 8, Clause 7 to justify their federal building project. But did either the Framers or the Ratifying Conventions anticipate such activity, or was this a creation of ambitious politicians bent on bringing the pork home to their constituents after the Constitution was ratified? From the evidence, it was the latter.

On 4 September 1787, James McHenry of Maryland remarked in his journal written during the Philadelphia Convention, "Upon looking over the constitution it does not appear that the national legislature can *erect light houses* or *clean out or preserve the navigation of harbours....*"[108] McHenry thought it should, and two days later spoke to Nathaniel Gorham of Massachusetts and

Gouverneur Morris and Thomas Fitzimmons of Pennsylvania about the issue. Morris and Fitzimmons agreed with McHenry, with Morris suggesting that the Congress could do so under the "General Welfare Clause." McHenry then wrote, "If this comprehends such a power, it goes to authorise the legisl. to grant exclusive privileges to trading companies etc...."[109] Such a power to grant monopolies would have been rejected by the Southern States. In the final days of the Convention, Benjamin Franklin addressed the issue.

Franklin proposed adding, "to provide for cutting canals where deemed necessary" after the words "post roads" in Article I, Section 8, Clause 7. He was seconded by James Wilson and had the support of the entire Pennsylvania delegation. Roger Sherman objected to the motion and contended that "the expense, in such cases, will fall on the United States, and the benefit accrue to the places where the canals may be cut." Wilson refuted this claim and insisted it was "necessary to prevent a *state* from obstructing the *general* welfare." Rufus King of Massachusetts supported Sherman's objection and added that if the general government could cut canals, some would then say it can also establish regional banks and mercantile monopolies to assist in such work, policies that would sharply divide the States.[110]

Wilson then made perhaps the most striking statement of the Convention and in essence laid the groundwork for the "implied powers" of the Constitution. "As to banks, [Wilson] did not think, with Mr. King, that the power, in that point of view, would excite the prejudices and parties apprehended. As to mercantile monopolies, *they are already included in the power to regulate trade*" (emphasis added). George Mason said he was "for limiting the power to the single case of canals. *He was afraid of monopolies of every sort, which he did not think were by any means already implied by the Constitution, as supposed by Mr. Wilson*" (emphasis added). Franklin's motion on canals was voted down 8 to 3, and would not have received those three votes if the motion had gone beyond mere canal-cutting.[111]

Madison called the power to establish post roads "harmless" in Federalist No. 42, and granted that the States had exclusive jurisdiction over their "internal order, improvement, and prosperity" in Federalist No. 45.[112] Tench Coxe of Pennsylvania, an ardent supporter of the Constitution, expanded on the theme. Writing as "A Freeman" in 1788, he said:

> [The general government] cannot interfere with the opening of rivers and canals; the making or regulation of roads, except post roads; building bridges; erecting ferries; establishment of state seminaries of learning; libraries; literary, religious, trading or manufacturing societies; erecting or regulating the police of cities, towns or boroughs; creating new state offices, building light houses, public wharves, county gaols [jails], markets, or other public buildings…nor can they do any other matter or thing appertaining to the internal affairs of any state, whether legislative, executive or judicial, civil or ecclesiastical.[113]

And later, as to the power of the States in this regard, Coxe wrote:

> The several states can create corporations civil and religious; prohibit or impose duties on the importation of

slaves into their own ports; establish seminaries of learning; erect boroughs, cities and counties; promote and establish manufacturers; open roads; clear rivers; cut canals; regulate descents and marriages; licence taverns…establish ferries; erect public buildings…establish poor houses, hospitals, and houses of employment; regulate the police; and many other things of the utmost importance to the happiness of their respective citizens. *In short, besides the particulars enumerated, every thing of a domestic nature must or can be done by them.*[114] (emphasis added)

While on the floor of Congress in 1791, Madison said that "he well recollected that a power to grant charters of incorporations had been proposed in the General Convention and rejected." The following year, Hamilton countered that "it must be confessed, however, that very different accounts are given the import of the proposition, and of the motives for rejecting it. Some affirm that it was confined to the opening of canals and obstructions in rivers; others, that it embraced banks; and others, that it extended to the power of incorporating generally. Some, again, allege that it was disagreed to because it was thought improper to vest in Congress a power of erecting corporations. Others, because it was thought unnecessary to *specify* the power, and inexpedient to furnish an additional topic of objection to the Constitution. In this state of the matter, no inference whatever can be drawn from it."[115] Of course, Madison's journal of the Convention would not be public for another thirty years, but from the record it is clear that Hamilton may have been stretching the truth a bit, particularly in regard to the idea that the power was rejected because some thought it was unwise to "*specify* the power."

Abraham Baldwin of Georgia, in relaying to Thomas Jefferson a conversation he had with James Wilson in 1791, put an exclamation point on the issue. Baldwin reminded Wilson that during the Convention, the power to "erect corporations" was "struck out." And though several other powers were proposed, such as the power to establish a bank, the Convention rejected the idea outright. Gouverneur Morris, in fact, thought that "it was extremely doubtful whether the constitution they were framing could ever be passed at all by the people of America; that to give it its best chance, however, they should make it as palatable as possible, and put nothing into it *not very essential*.... Whereupon it was rejected, as was every other special power, except that of giving copyrights to authors, and patents to inventors; the general power of incorporating being whittled down to this shred. Wilson agreed to the fact."[116]

As a whole, at the time the Constitution was ratified, the founding generation understood that the Constitution did not grant the general government the power to incorporate, grant monopolies, or build "internal improvements," and that the powers over "domestic happiness" were left to the State governments. Post roads were limited, and no other clause in the Constitution granted the general government indefinite power to spend money on domestic projects that benefited one State, county, or city at the expense of the whole. This is why during their presidencies, both James Madison and James Monroe vetoed "internal improvement" bills and instructed Congress to write a constitutional amendment authorizing such power. Unfortunately, such fiscal restraint has been ignored by successive generations of Washington politicians. Roads in small town U.S.A. are often improved with dollars from the general government, and Congress has created dozens of government corporations since the early days of the progressive era in the 1900s. According to the Constitution *as ratified*, all of this is unconstitutional.

War Powers

"To declare War, grant Letters of Marque and Reprisal, and make Rules concerning Captures on Land and Water;

"To raise and support Armies, but no Appropriation of Money to that Use shall be for a longer Term than two Years;

"To provide and maintain a Navy;

"To make Rules for the Government and Regulation of the land and naval Forces;

"To provide for calling forth the Militia to execute the Laws of the Union, suppress Insurrections and repel Invasions;

"To provide for organizing, arming, and disciplining, the Militia, and for governing such Part of them as may be employed in the Service of the United States, reserving to the States respectively, the Appointment of the Officers, and the Authority of training the Militia according to the discipline prescribed by Congress."
Article I, Section 8, Clauses 11–16.

According to the Constitution, Congress alone has the power to declare war. This power faced little debate during the Philadelphia Convention, and most of the founding generation believed vesting this power in the popular branch of government was preferable to handing over the military to the executive. The other war powers clauses, however, were more contentious. There was substantial opposition to a standing army, and many opponents of the Constitution questioned central control of the State militias. This fear was born from their experiences in the American War for Independence, in which the colonial militias formed the first armies against the British regulars; had the militias been under direct British authority, the war might have taken a very different turn. The militias were designed to protect the people of the States. The Second Amendment to the Constitution—"A well-regulated militia, being necessary to the security of a free state, the right of the people to keep and bear arms, shall not be infringed"—was added in large part as a State check on the power, given the expansive war powers clauses, of the general government.

On 17 August 1787, John Dickinson moved that Congress should have the power to "make war." Charles Pinckney opposed giving this power to the lower house. In his drafts for a new Constitution, Pinckney proposed to vest this power in the Senate. He reasoned that the Senate, as the representatives of the States and "being more acquainted with foreign affairs" would better safeguard the power of war and peace. His colleague from South Carolina, Pierce Butler, argued that the executive should have the power to "make war." Elbridge Gerry was shocked, and declared he "never expected to hear in a republic a motion to empower the Executive alone to declare war." Both Gerry and Madison moved to replace "make" with "declare" but supported the executive having the power to "repel sudden attacks." George Mason summarized the general sentiment of the delegates when he said that he did not trust giving the executive or the Senate the power of war.

"He was for clogging rather than facilitating war; but for facilitating peace." Most also agreed that "declare" was a narrower term than "make," and thus limited the power of Congress.[117]

"Brutus" wrote in 1788 that the American war powers should differ from their European brethren. "The European governments are almost all of them framed, and administered, with a view to arms, and war, as that in which their chief glory consists; they mistake the end of government—it was designed to save mens [sic] lives, not to destroy them. We ought to furnish the world with an example of a great people, who in their civil institutions hold chiefly in view, the attainment of virtue, and happiness among ourselves."[118] The founding generation desired peace, but these men also understood that security demanded the power to wage war, if necessary. As Madison argued in Federalist No. 41, "Security against foreign danger is one of the primitive objects of civil society.... The powers requisite for attaining it, must be effectually confided to the foederal councils."[119]

Here was the rub. Not everyone believed that the general government should have unlimited power over "the sword." The Articles of Confederation granted Congress the power to declare war, but the States had a primary role in the process. "Brutus," in fact, lamented that the Constitution placed the militia under the control of the general government, because this removed a State's independent ability to repel an invasion. Many feared the effect a standing army would have on society.

Richard Henry Lee wrote that the presence of a standing army "constantly terminated in the destruction of liberty...."[120] Of course, by standing army, Lee was referring to a professional class of soldiers paid by the treasury and permanently garrisoned, even in peace. During the Philadelphia Convention, Elbridge Gerry called a standing army "dangerous to liberty" and wished for restrictions on both the number of men in service and the length of time in which they would serve. George Mason called the "absolute" prohibition of a standing army unsafe, but he still argued that there should be some guard against the potential "danger of them." Gerry and Mason were in the minority at the Convention, but Gerry knew that the general public would not be as inclined toward a professional army as the delegates in Philadelphia.[121]

James Wilson began public debate over the Constitution with a speech in the Philadelphia State House Yard on 6 October 1787. He anticipated several attacks on the Constitution, including those against a standing army, and his comments would be fodder for opponents throughout 1787 and 1788. Wilson contended that a standing army was an absolute necessity for the United States, for he "did not know a nation in the world, which has not found it necessary and useful to maintain the appearance of strength in a season of most profound tranquility."[122] Wilson, though, sold the possibility of a standing army by insisting that the Constitution provided ample "control" and "restrictions" over the military force.

Richard Henry Lee was the first to go on the offensive in the Federal Farmer No. 3. "I see so many men in America fond of a standing army, and especially among those who probably will have a large share in administering the federal system; it is very evident to me, that we shall have a large standing army as soon as the monies to support them can be possibly found." He insinuated that these men represented a class of parasites and that the only way to check the harm and expense of a professional military was through the States.[123]

A writer under the name "A Democratic Federalist" called Wilson's defense of a standing army "a threadbare hackneyed argument, which has been answered over and over in different ages and does not deserve even the smallest consideration.... Had we a standing army when the British invaded our peaceful shores? Was it a standing army that gained the battle of Lexington and Bunker's Hill, and took the ill-fated [John] Burgoyne? Is not a well-regulated militia sufficient for every purpose of internal defense?"[124] A pamphlet written by "A Federal Republican" which appeared in Philadelphia newspapers in November 1787 called a standing army "the grand machine made use of to subvert the liberties of free states." The writer also surmised, "If therefore the government of the United States be just and equal, and the states are to retain their separate powers, a standing army is useless and dangerous. It will inevitably sow the seeds of corruption and depravity of manners."[125]

Alexander Hamilton warned, in Federalist No. 8, that if the Constitution was rejected, standing armies would be "inevitable" because the States would form two or three potentially mutually hostile "confederacies" in North America. United under the Constitution, however, standing armies might not be necessary. "If we are wise enough to preserve the Union, we may for ages enjoy an advantage similar to that of an insulated nation.... Extensive military establishments cannot, in this position, be necessary to our security."[126] It was a clever argument that put his opponents on the defensive by portraying them as disunionists (which they weren't, but it made for useful propaganda).

During the Pennsylvania Ratifying Convention, Wilson followed a similar track, arguing that while the Constitution allowed for Congress to raise a standing army during peace, it would do so in a responsible and limited way. "I believe the *power* of raising and keeping up an army, in time of peace, is essential to every government. No government can secure its citizens against dangers, internal and external, without possessing it, and sometimes carrying it into execution. I confess it is a power in the exercise of which all wise and moderate governments will be as prudent and forbearing as possible." The ability to have an army, Wilson added, would place the United States in a position of strength. Thus, "Our enemies, finding us invulnerable, will not attack us; and we shall thus prevent the occasion for larger standing armies."[127] Hamilton and "Brutus" exchanged barbs over the issue in December 1787 and January 1788. Hamilton dedicated Federalist Nos. 23 to 26, which appeared over a five day span in December 1787, to congressional war powers. In Federalist No. 25, Hamilton said, "If to obviate this consequence, it should be resolved to extend the prohibition to the *raising* of armies in time of peace, the United States would then exhibit the most extraordinary spectacle, which the world has yet seen—that of a nation incapacitated by its constitution to prepare for defence, before it was actually invaded."[128]

Moreover, Hamilton emphasized that Congress had to re-evaluate the necessity of a standing army every two years. "The Legislature of the United States will be *obliged* by this provision, once at least in every two years, to deliberate upon the propriety of keeping a military force on foot; to come to a new resolution on the point; and to declare their sense of the matter, by a formal vote in the face of their constituents. They are not *at liberty* to vest in the executive department permanent funds for the support of an army; if they were even incautious enough to be willing to repose in it so improper a confidence."[129]

"Brutus" wasn't sold. In a scathing rebuttal, he called Hamilton's arguments sophomoric and circular:

From the positive, and dogmatic manner, in which this author delivers his opinions, and answers objections made to his sentiments—one would conclude, that he was some pedantic pedagogue who had been accustomed to deliver his dogmas to pupils, who always placed implicit faith in what he delivered.... But, why is this provision so ridiculous? because, says this author, it is unnecessary. But, why is it unnecessary? "because, the principles and habits, as well as the power of the Americans are directly opposed to standing armies; and there is as little necessity to guard against them by positive constitutions, as to prohibit the establishment of the Mahometan religion." It is admitted then, that a standing army in time of peace, is an evil. I ask then, why should this government be authorised to do evil? If the principles and habits of the people of this country are opposed to standing armies in time of peace, if they do not contribute to the public good, but would endanger the public liberty and happiness, why should the government be vested with the power? No reason can be given, why rulers should be authorised to do, what, if done, would oppose the principles and habits of the people, and endanger the public safety, but there is every reason in the world, that they should be prohibited from the exercise of such a power.[130]

By the time the State ratifying conventions of Massachusetts, Virginia, and North Carolina met, the issue had been thoroughly dissected, but this didn't stop delegates from debating the issue. It was that important. Thomas Dawes Jr. reminded the Massachusetts Ratifying Convention that congressional war powers under the Constitution were in large part borrowed from the English declaration of rights, while his colleague Theodore Sedgwick insisted that "every possible provision against an abuse of power" had been made in the Constitution.[131] James Iredell of North Carolina argued that the "power is absolutely necessary, and must be vested somewhere; that it can be vested nowhere so well as in the general government." Plus, the power was restricted by the language of the clause, which as Hamilton noted required Congress to vote on military appropriations every two years.[132]

George Mason warned the Virginia Ratifying Convention that "once a standing army is established in any country, the people lose their liberty. When, against a regular and disciplined army, yeomanry are the only defence,—yeomanry, unskilful and unarmed,—what chance is there for preserving freedom?" Madison suggested in response that the best way to "guard against a standing army, is to render it unnecessary." How could the Constitution do that? "Give the general government full power to call forth the militia, and exert the whole natural strength of the Union, when necessary."[133] But that, of course, only raised the fear of central control of the State militias.

The power of the sword was most dreaded in relation to its effect on State sovereignty. Article I, Section 8, Clauses 15 and 16 place the "organizing, arming, and disciplining" of the militia in the hands of the general government, and they authorize Congress to call up the militia to "execute the Laws of the Union, suppress Insurrections and repel Invasions." Opponents believed the clauses would render a State unable to defend itself against either foreign danger or the general government. They viewed it as another attempt at consolidation and insisted that proponents of the Constitution explain why these clauses were inserted in the document. Early in the Philadelphia Convention, Madison objected to a clause that would have allowed the central government to use force against a "delinquent state." He said that "the more he reflected on the use of force, the more he doubted the practicability, the justice and the efficacy of it when applied to people collectively and not individually. A union of the states containing such an ingredient seemed to provide for its own destruction. The use of force against a State, would look more like a declaration of war, than an infliction of punishment, and would probably be considered by the party attacked as a dissolution of all previous compacts by which it might be bound."[134] The clause was postponed and brought up later in the Convention under different language, but Madison made it clear, and was seconded by Elbridge Gerry, that a State could not be coerced by the general government; most of the Framers agreed.

William Paterson of New Jersey is remembered for presenting the "Small State Plan" or "New Jersey Plan," which would have created a unicameral legislature with each State getting one vote. Often forgotten is that his plan—designed to amend the Articles of Confederation rather than create an entirely new Constitution—also empowered the executive to use the military to "compel an obedience" to federal law. Robert Yates of New York remarked in his journal that Paterson told him, "No government could be energetic on paper only, which was no more than straw…and…that there must be a small standing force to give every government weight."[135] While favoring equal representation for the States, he was not opposed to a strong central authority and did not fear either a standing army or central control of the militias. In that regard, his plan was more nationalist than Madison's bicameral Virginia Plan that based representation on state population. The New Jersey and Virginia Plans led of course to the Great Compromise on popular and State representation. But not included in that compromise was any grant to the general government to "compel an obedience" by military force.

The Convention implicitly discussed this issue in August. An early draft of the Constitution allowed the general government "To subdue a rebellion in any State, on the application of its legislature." Luther Martin of Maryland immediately objected and said he "opposed it as giving a dangerous & unnecessary power." Elbridge Gerry of Massachusetts remarked that he was "against letting loose the myrmidons of the U. States on a State without its own consent. The States would be the best Judges in such cases. More blood would have been spilt in Massachusetts in the late insurrection [Shay's Rebellion], if the General authority had intermeddled." Gouverneur Morris, however, could not understand the apprehension, and remarked, "We are acting a very strange part. We first form a strong man to protect us, and at the same time wish to tie his hands behind him." The clause was defeated in a close vote (with the majority obviously reluctant to authorize military force to coerce a State),[136] which tied into the fear of some delegates about giving the general government control of the militia, because it would make the States impotent *if* the general government *did* try to coerce a State.

When the issue of central control of the militia came up for debate in August, John Dickinson said, "We are come now to a most important matter, that of the sword." He did not think the States would "give up all authority over the Militia." Oliver Ellsworth concurred. "The whole authority over the Militia ought by no means to be taken away from the States whose consequence would pine away to nothing after such a sacrifice of power.... It must be vain to ask the States to give the Militia out of their hands." Roger Sherman argued that the States would want to retain control of the Militia to not only protect against "invasions and insurrections," but also to enforce "obedience to their laws." Gerry, in true pessimistic form, "thought this is the last point remaining to be surrendered [by the States]. If it be agreed to by the Convention, the plan will have as black a mark as was set on Cain. [Gerry] had no such confidence in the General Government as some Gentlemen possessed, and believed it would be found that the States have not."[137]

Madison disagreed, suggesting that "if the States would trust the General Government with a power over the public treasure, they would from the same consideration of necessity grant it the direction of the public force. Those who had a full view of the public situation would from a sense of the danger, guard against it; the States would not be separately impressed with the general situation, nor have the due confidence in the concurrent exertions of each other." Charles Pinckney of South Carolina went so far as to suggest that the militia were useless for the common defense of the Union. He preferred a strong standing army. "The United States had been making an experiment without it, and we see the consequences in their rapid approaches toward anarchy."[138]

As the Convention continued debate on clauses 15 and 16 a few days later, proponents attempted to pour cold water on the flames of opposition. They had some—but by no means universal—success. Elbridge Gerry said that these clauses, particularly clause 16, reduced the States to mere "drill-sergeants" and thought that the people of the States would regard this as a "system of Despotism." Rufus King, though, explained that "*organizing...*meant, proportioning the officers and men…*arming*, specifying the kind, size and caliber of arms…*disciplining* prescribing the manual exercise evolutions &c." Madison said that he understood the language to mean that the States still furnished the arms and punished the men, but King said that "*arming*" also "included authority to regulate the modes of furnishing" weapons. As a result, Oliver Ellsworth and Roger Sherman argued for removing that power, the object being "to refer the plan for the Militia to the General Government but leave the execution of it to the State Governments." John Langdon of New Hampshire responded that "he could not understand the jealousy expressed by some Gentlemen. The General & State Governments were not enemies to each other, but different institutions for the good of the people of America…. In transferring power from one to the other—I only take out of my left hand what it cannot so well use, and put it into my right hand where it can be better used."[139]

Gerry retorted that central control of the militia was "rather taking out of the right hand and putting it into the left. Will any man say that liberty will be as safe in the hands of eighty or a hundred men taken from the whole continent, as in the hands of two or three hundred taken from a single State?" Jonathan Dayton of New Jersey agreed, for "uniformity" would never be possible in the United States. Luther Martin believed "the States would never give up the power over the Militia." Madison, however, foreshadowed the defense of the two clauses when he said at the conclusion of the day-long debate, "As the greatest danger is that of disunion of the States, it is necessary to guard against it by sufficient powers to the Common Government and as the greatest danger to liberty is from large standing armies, it is best to prevent them by an effectual provision for a good Militia."[140]

Opponents fired their first salvo against congressional control of the militia on 29 November 1787. Luther Martin appeared before the Maryland Legislature and opined that the general government would resort to force should a State refuse to cooperate. This, he said, will involve "the whole Militia of any State…a power, which it was vainly urged ought never to exceed a certain proportion. By organizing the Militia Congress have taken the whole power from the State Governments; and by…encreasing the Standing Army, their power will increase…."[141] On the same day, "Brutus" wrote in the *New York Journal* that:

> If then this government should not derive support from the good will of the people, it must be executed by force, or not executed at all; either case would lead to the total destruction of liberty.—The convention seemed aware of this, and have therefore provided for calling out the militia to execute the laws of the union. If this system was so framed as to command that respect from the people, which every good free government will obtain, this provision was unnecessary—the people would support the civil magistrate. This power is a novel one, in free governments—these have depended for the execution of the laws on the Posse Comitatus, and never raised an idea, that the people would refuse to aid the civil magistrate in executing those laws they themselves had made.[142]

James Wilson attempted to silence critics of this power by mocking them. This was not uncommon. He was called "James de Caledonia" as a slap at his haughty nature, and he often peered condescendingly over his wire rimmed glasses at opponents. On 11 December 1787, Wilson said, "I believe any gentleman, who possesses military experience, will inform you that men without a uniformity of arms, accoutrements, and discipline, are no more than a mob in a camp; that, in the field, instead of assisting, they interfere with one another...." Of course, he insinuated that his *own* military experience lent to this observation; yet, his military experience was confined to defending himself against a group of armed opponents in 1779 at his house in Philadelphia. He did not serve in the War for Independence and only reluctantly supported the cause. No matter, he appealed to "military experience for the truth" of his observations and remarked that these clauses in the Constitution were "calculated to produce good effects. How powerful and respectable must the body of militia appear under general and uniform regulations! How disjointed, weak, and inefficient are they at present!"[143]

Alexander Hamilton had more authority on such matters due to his solid military background. He wrote Federalist No. 29 to defend central power over the militia. Hamilton called this the "natural incidents to the duties of superintending the common defence" and wondered how anyone could object. Like Wilson, Hamilton spoke down to his opponents. "It requires no skill in the science of war," he said, "to discern that uniformity in the organization and discipline of the militia would be attended with the most beneficial effects, whenever they were called into service for the public defence." Plus, Hamilton could not grasp his opponents' arguments:

> Of the different grounds which have been taken in opposition to the plan of the Convention, there is none

that was so little to have been expected, or is so untenable in itself, as the one from which this particular provision has been attacked. If a well regulated militia be the most natural defence of a free country, it ought certainly to be under the regulation and at the disposal of that body which is constituted the guardian of the national security. If standing armies are dangerous to liberty, an efficacious power over the militia, in the body to whose care the protection of the State is committed, ought as far as possible to take away the inducement and the pretext to such unfriendly institutions. If the foederal government can command the aid of the militia in those emergencies which call for the military arm in support of the civil magistrate, it can the better dispense with the employment of a different kind of force. If it cannot avail itself of the former, it will be obliged to recur to the latter. To render an army unnecessary will be a more certain method of preventing its existence than a thousand prohibitions upon paper.[144]

Hamilton said that reading tracts against the Constitution was like "perusing some ill written tale or romance; which instead of natural and agreeable images exhibits to the mind nothing but frightful and distorted shapes—Gorgons Hydras and Chimeras dire—discoloring and disfiguring whatever it represents and trans-forming every thing it touches into a monster." He could not coun-tenance how opponents of the Constitution feared central power over the militia when the States ultimately controlled it through the "*sole and exclusive appointment of the officers....* If it were pos-sible seriously to indulge a jealousy of the militia upon any conceivable establishment under the Foederal Government, the circumstance of the officers being in the appointment of the States ought at once to extinguish it. There can be no doubt that this circumstance will always secure to them a preponderating influence over the militia."[145] After that, Hamilton could never foresee a time when the militia would be used to coerce a State.

During the Connecticut Ratifying Convention, Oliver Ellsworth argued that the Constitution needed a "coercive principle." But, "The only question is, Shall it be a coercion of law, or a coercion of arms?" If the people of the States refused to abide by a "coercion of law," the result would be, in his opinion, "a war of the states one against the other." As a result, Ellsworth said he was for "coercion by law—that coercion which acts only upon delinquent individuals. *This Constitution does not attempt to coerce sovereign bodies, states, in their political capacity*. No coercion is applicable to such bodies, but that of an armed force. If we should attempt to execute the laws of the Union by sending an armed force against a delinquent state, it would involve the good and the bad, the innocent and the guilty, in the same calamity"[146] (emphasis added).

Ellsworth was simply restating what the majority of the founding generation believed: States would never be coerced by a domestic military force. Yet, regardless of what Hamilton and Wilson said, opponents were more perceptive about the potential abuse of that power, with the end result being the loss of 600,000 men between 1861 and 1865 in a war of coercion against the Southern States. But in fairness, with the exception of the years between 1861 and 1877, the American standing army never reached significant numbers until well into the twentieth century. As proponents suggested, the militia generally prevented the need for one.

Necessary and Proper

"To make all Laws which shall be necessary and proper for carrying into Execution the foregoing Powers, and all other Powers vested by this Constitution in the Government of the United States, or in any Department or Officer thereof." **Article I, Section 8, Clause 18.**

No other clause in Article I, Section 8 received as much attention during the ratifying debates as the "Necessary and Proper Clause." Opponents argued, and often rightly so, that the clause would be used to expand the powers of the general government beyond those enumerated or delegated in Article I, Section 8. Alexander Hamilton did just that in 1791 by defending the incorporation of a central banking system. He admitted that the ability to incorporate a bank was not listed in the Constitution, but that it could be inferred through the "Necessary and Proper Clause." John Marshall followed up in 1819 by defending Hamilton's so-called "loose construction" theory in the *McCullough v. Maryland* decision. To paraphrase, Marshall argued that as long as the ends justified the means, and the law was within the letter and spirit of the Constitution, the general government could do virtually anything it pleased. These two opinions have been cited as *the* definitive statements on the intent of the "Necessary and Proper Clause," but such language was rejected during the debates leading to ratification in 1787 and 1788.

There was little debate on the "Necessary and Proper Clause" during the Philadelphia Convention. On 15 September, George Mason referenced it in his speech against the Constitution. He called it the "general clause" and said that because of it, "the

Congress may grant monopolies in trade and commerce, constitute new crimes, inflict unusual and severe punishments, and extend their powers as far as they shall think proper; so that the State legislatures have no security for the powers now presumed to remain to them, or the people for their rights."[147] Elbridge Gerry made a similar statement and argued that the "rights of the Citizens were…rendered insecure…by the general power of the Legislature to make what laws they may please to call necessary and proper…."[148] These arguments set a general trend and ultimately put proponents of the Constitution on the defensive.

While not mentioning the clause by name, James Wilson addressed the issue in his famous "State House Yard" speech on 6 October 1787. Wilson said, "But in delegating federal powers, another criterion was necessarily introduced, and the congressional authority is to be collected, not from tacit implication, but from the positive grant expressed in the instrument of union…everything which is not given [as an explicit power to Congress] is reserved [to the States or to the people]."[149] Simply put, Wilson rejected Mason's claim that the "Necessary and Proper Clause" or any other "general clause" of the Constitution created "implied powers." Powers were expressly granted, and if the Constitution did not grant a power to the general government, it was "reserved" to the people of the States.

On 12 October 1787, the "Federal Farmer" warned of the potential for Congress to abuse the "Necessary and Proper Clause." "In making laws to carry those powers into effect, it is to be expected, that a wise and prudent congress will pay respect to the opinions of a free people, and bottom their laws on those principles which have been considered as essential and fundamental in the British, and in our government: But a congress of a different character will not be bound by the constitution to pay respect to those principles." Based on his understanding of human nature and history, the "Federal Farmer" had little hope of congressional restraint. "But the general presumption being, that men who govern, will, in doubtful cases, construe laws and constitutions most favourably for encreasing their own powers...."[150]

"An Old Whig" specifically addressed Wilson's language on 17 October 1787. "If *this* [Wilson's description] be a just representation of the matter, the authority of the several states will be sufficient to protect our liberties from the encroachments of Congress, without any continental bill of rights; *unless* the powers which are *expressly given* to Congress are *too large*." The "Old Whig" thought that was the case. He called the powers contained in the clause "*undefined, unbounded, and immense*" and questioned, "Under such a clause as this can any thing be said to be reserved and kept back from Congress? Can it be said that the Congress have no power but what *is expressed*? 'To make all laws which shall be necessary and proper' is in other words to make all such laws which *the Congress shall think necessary and proper*...." The "Old Whig" lamented that the only check on this power would be force, either internal or external, a calamity "which every good man would wish his country at all times to be delivered from." Ultimately, the "Old Whig" concluded if Congress could determine its own power "in all cases whatsoever" then this dangerous clause needed to be eliminated or Congress needed a check on this authority.[151]

"Brutus," meanwhile, feared that with the "Necessary and Proper" clause, "This government is to possess absolute and uncontroulable power, legislative, executive and judicial, with respect to every object to which it extends...." The ultimate effect, in his opinion, would be the annihilation of the State governments and the reduction of

> this country to one single government. And if they may
> do it, it is pretty certain they will; for it will be found
> that the power retained by the individual states, small
> as it is, will be a cog upon the wheels of the government
> of the United States; the latter therefore will be natu-
> rally inclined to remove it out of the way. Besides, it is
> a truth confirmed by the unerring experience of ages,
> that every man, and every body of men, invested with
> power, are ever disposed to increase it, and to acquire
> a superiority over every thing that stands in their way.
> This disposition, which is implanted in human nature,
> will operate in the federal legislature to lessen and ulti-
> mately subvert the state authority."[152]

James Wilson responded to his critics during the Pennsylvania Ratifying Convention. He could not fathom how opponents of the Constitution viewed the "Necessary and Proper Clause" as an indefinite grant of power. The clause, he suggested, "gives no more or other powers" than those enumerated in Article I, Section 8. "It is saying no more than that the powers we have already particularly given, shall be effectually carried into execution."[153] Edmund Randolph reassured his colleagues at the Virginia Ratifying Convention that the clause "did not in the least increase the powers of Congress." Randolph additionally said that if Congress should exceed the powers delegated to it in the Constitution, it would be an "absolute usurpation," and "the influence of the state governments will nip it in the bud of hope."[154]

Archibald Maclaine of North Carolina echoed Randolph when he said during the State's First Ratifying Convention, "If Congress should make a law beyond the powers and the spirit of the Constitution, should we not say to Congress, 'You have no authority to make this law. There are limits beyond which you cannot go. You cannot exceed the power prescribed by the Constitution. You are amenable to us for your conduct. This act is unconstitutional. We will disregard it, and punish you for the attempt.'"[155] Randolph and Maclaine viewed the people of the States as the final arbiter in a dispute between the general and State governments.

Both Madison and Hamilton refuted attacks on the "Necessary and Proper" clause in *The Federalist Papers*. In Federalist No. 33, Hamilton called the language of those who lambasted the clause "virulent invective and petulant" and wrote they had used "exaggerated colours of misrepresentation, as the pernicious engines by which their local governments were to be destroyed and their liberties exterminated—as the hideous monster whose devouring jaws would spare neither sex nor age, nor high nor low, nor sacred nor profane…." Yet, Hamilton insisted that the government would be the same had the "Necessary and Proper" clause been omitted. He called it "only a declaratory of truth, which would have resulted by necessary and unavoidable implication from the very act of constituting a Foederal Government, and vesting it with certain specified powers."[156]

Madison, in Federalist No. 44, regarded the "Necessary and Proper" clause as essential to the spirit of the Constitution, for without it, "the whole Constitution would be a dead letter." Most important, Madison thought that by listing the clause, the Framers avoided potential abuse. "Had the Constitution been silent on this head, there can be no doubt that all the particular powers, requisite as means of executing the general powers, would have resulted to the government, by unavoidable implication."[157] Interestingly, Madison reasoned that *eliminating* the clause would lead to an "elastic" interpretation of congressional powers, whereas Marshall and later Hamilton insisted that the clause itself allowed for implication.

James Iredell of North Carolina, writing as "Marcus" in March 1788, said, "If Congress, under pretense of exercising the power delegated to them, should, in fact, by the exercise of any other power, usurp upon the rights of the different Legislatures, or of any private citizens, the people will be exactly in the same situation as if there had been an express provision against such power.... It would be an act of tyranny."[158] George Nicholas in the Virginia Ratifying Convention argued, "The clause which was affectedly called the *sweeping* clause contained no new grant of power ... if it had been added at the end of every one of the enumerated powers, instead of being inserted at the end of all, it would be obvious to any one that it was no augmentation of power.... As it would grant no new power if inserted at the end of each clause, it could not when subjoined to the whole."[159] That is how the majority of the founding generation viewed the "Necessary and Proper" clause. Certainly, opponents were perceptive when they believed the clause would be abused, but in 1787 and 1788, proponents of the Constitution made a good faith effort to calm disquiet over one of the "general phrases." Enough people believed them to ratify the Constitution. The standard and original interpretation of the "Necessary and Proper" clause was that it added no new or elastic powers to Congress, and that should be the way we interpret it today.

State Sovereignty

"No State shall enter into any Treaty, Alliance, or Confederation; grant Letters of Marque and Reprisal; coin Money; emit Bills of Credit; make any Thing but gold and silver Coin a Tender in Payment of Debts; pass any Bill of Attainder, ex post facto Law, or Law impairing the Obligation of Contracts, or grant any Title of Nobility.

"No State shall, without the Consent of the Congress, lay any Imposts or Duties on Imports or Exports, except what may be absolutely necessary for executing its inspection Laws: and the net Produce of all Duties and Imposts, laid by any State on Imports or Exports, shall be for the Use of the Treasury of the United States; and all such Laws shall be subject to the Revision and Controul of the Congress.

"No State shall, without the Consent of Congress, lay any duty of Tonnage, keep Troops, or Ships of War in time of Peace, enter into any Agreement or Compact with another State, or with a foreign Power, or engage in War, unless actually invaded, or in such imminent Danger as will not admit of delay." **Article I, Section 10.**

Article I, Section 10 delegated certain enumerated powers to the general government so they could be jointly exercised for the common good. The States, however, retained all other powers. That is how proponents argued the point during 1787 and 1788. They had to, because the chief argument against the Constitution was that its "general clauses" endangered State sovereignty and had within them the potential of subverting the States in favor of a centralized despotism; the Constitution's supporters had to reassure the doubters this wasn't the case.

When Thomas Jefferson concluded the Declaration of Independence with the following lines: "as Free and Independent States, they have full Power to levy War, conclude Peace, contract Alliances, establish Commerce, and to do all other Acts and Things which Independent States may of right do…" he defined the American "State." To Jefferson, a State was and is a sovereign political entity, equal to the "State of Great Britain." States had exclusive (sovereign) control of their diplomatic and commercial relations as well as "all other Acts and Things which Independent States may of right do." Those other "Acts and Things" included, but were not limited to, the promotion of domestic peace and tranquility and the protection of life, liberty, and property. So, according to the Constitution and Article I, Section 10, the States delegated their diplomatic powers and a portion of their commercial powers, but retained control of "all other Acts and Things." These powers were undefined and unlimited.

For virtually every State power delegated to the general government by Article I, Section 10, there was a corresponding enumeration in Article I, Section 8. The two Articles should be read in conjunction. For example, the general government had the power to declare war and handle foreign policy. Clauses 1 and 3 of Article I, Section 10 simply reaffirmed that fact by stating, "No State shall enter into any Treaty, Alliance, or Confederation; grant Letters of Marque and Reprisal…" and "No State shall, without the Consent of Congress…keep Troops, or Ships of War in time of Peace, enter into any Agreement or Compact with another State, or with a foreign Power, or engage in War, unless actually invaded, or in such imminent Danger as will not admit of delay." States could maintain a militia, but the general government had the authority to raise a professional army and navy.

The general government, through the "Commerce Clause" of Article I, Section 8, controlled foreign trade, but the States retained the right to regulate intrastate commerce, including the promotion of agriculture and manufacturing. Both the general government and the State governments could levy taxes, but the States could not "coin Money; emit Bills of Credit; make any Thing but gold and silver Coin a Tender in Payment of Debts...." Thus, though the State governments delegated some of their commercial sovereignty, they retained a substantial portion of it, particularly in regard to domestic production. This is how proponents argued the point during the ratification debates.

One common argument against the Constitution centered on the general government's authority to tax. Not only were opponents worried that it would use the power of the purse to squeeze the people of the States, they worried that the States, by default, forfeited that power. For example, in November 1787 "An Old Whig" wrote that "if the Legislature of the United States shall possess the powers of internal as well as external taxation, the individual states in their separate capacities, will be less than the shadows of a name..." and concluded, "We ought to be very fully convinced of an absolute necessity existing before we entrust the whole power of taxation to the hands of Congress; and the moment we do so, we ought by consent to annihilate the individual states; for the powers of the individual states will be as effectually swallowed as a drop of water in the ocean; and the next consequence will be a speedy dissolution of our republican form of government."[160]

But there is no such prohibition on State taxation in Article I, Section 10, as proponents illustrated. Alexander Hamilton argued in Federalist No. 34 that "the particular States, under the proposed Constitution…have CO-EQUAL authority with the Union in the article of revenue, except as to duties on imports. As this leaves open to the States far the greatest part of the resources of the community, there can be no color for the assertion, that they would not possess means, as abundant as could be desired, for the supply of their own wants, independent of all external control."[161] Oliver Ellsworth, at the Connecticut Ratifying Convention, charged that the power to tax was not "exclusively" confined to the general government. "It does not say that Congress shall have all these sources of revenue, and the states none. All, excepting the impost, still lie open to the states. This state owes a debt; it must provide for the payment of it. So do all the other states. This will not escape the attention of Congress."[162] The consensus, then, among proponents, was that if the Constitution was silent on the issue or power, the States retained control or at minimum concurrent jurisdiction over such matters.

Other powers prohibited to the States were also denied to the general government. Neither the general government nor the States could, for example, pass bills of attainder, ex post facto laws, or titles of nobility. The powers delegated to the general government in Article I, Section 10 were few, and proponents consistently underlined that fact during the ratification process. When Roger Sherman and Oliver Ellsworth transmitted a copy of the Constitution to Connecticut's governor in September 1787, they emphasized that the powers "vested in congress…extend only to matters respecting the common interests of the union, and are specially defined, so that the particular states retain their sovereignty in all other matters."[163] That is how the majority of the founding generation understood the Constitution and the powers of Congress vis-à-vis the States.

CHAPTER 3

The Executive Branch

In 2008, mother Peggy Joseph and her kids attended a campaign rally for then candidate Barack Obama in Sarasota, Florida. Following Obama's speech, Joseph said, "It was the most memorable time of my life. It was a touching moment, because I never thought this day would ever happen. I won't have to worry about puttin' gas in my car, I won't have to worry about payin' my mortgage, you know, if I help him, he's gonna help me." While laughable (and sad), this type of thinking is indicative of the modern public image of the president. Americans generally believe the president can solve problems in education, health care, jobs, wages, mortgages, gasoline prices, and a host of other domestic issues. Additionally, most Americans probably think the president has sole discretion over foreign policy and the decisions of war and peace. They are wrong on all accounts.

The president has, unfortunately, become the central figure in American politics. Since 1960, voter turnout in presidential election years is typically twenty points higher than in mid-term elections. Even the phrase "mid-term" is a by-product of the laser-beam focus Americans have on the executive branch. Americans commonly ignore the role of State and local governments in the American polity, they don't vote in State and local elections, and they barely turn out for "mid-term" congressional elections.

This is not the way the Founders viewed American government. The executive was not meant to be the dominant branch of the general government, Congress was. The executive branch was not meant to interfere in State and local affairs—indeed, State and local governments jealously guarded their prerogatives from a general government, let alone the executive branch, whose powers were meant to be strictly limited. The Founders would never have supported an executive branch that could rule by decree, and the Constitution *as ratified* does not allow for unrestrained executive authority. Returning the executive branch to its proper role should be the primary focus of all Americans who want a return to constitutional government.

The President

"The executive Power shall be vested in a President of the United States of America. He shall hold his Office during the Term of four Years....

"No person except a natural born Citizen, or a Citizen of the United States, at the time of the Adoption of this Constitution, shall be eligible to the Office of President; neither shall any Person be eligible to that Office who shall not have attained to the Age of thirty-five Years, and been fourteen Years a Resident within the United States....

"The President shall, at stated Times, receive for his Services, a Compensation, which shall neither be increased nor diminished during the Period for which he shall have been elected, and he shall not receive within that Period any other Emolument from the United States, or any of them." **Article II, Section 1, Clauses 1, 5, and 7.**

"The President, Vice President and all civil Officers of the United States, shall be removed from Office on Impeachment for, and Conviction of, Treason, Bribery, or other high Crimes and Misdemeanors." **Article II, Section 4.**

One of the fundamental differences between the Articles of Confederation and the Constitution is the executive branch; the president under the Articles of Confederation merely presided over Congress; there was no executive branch. Virtually every proposed revision of the Articles called for a separate executive. Madison's Virginia Plan called for a "national executive" to be elected by the "national legislature." Charles Pinckney's draft of a Constitution for the United States said, "The executive power of the United States shall be vested in a President of the United States of America, which shall be his style; and his title shall be His Excellency." William Paterson's New Jersey Plan would have instituted a plural "federal executive."[1] The lack of an executive was deemed one of the glaring deficiencies of the Articles of Confederation, but at the same time, many of the Founders were wary of a strong executive, and most Americans were not willing to create a virtual "king of the United States."

Pinckney, in fact, said during the Philadelphia Convention that he was "for a vigorous executive, but was afraid the executive powers of the existing Congress might extend to peace and war, &c.; which would render the executive a monarchy of the worst kind, to wit, an elective one."[2] When James Wilson moved that the executive should "consist of a single person," the Convention sat in silence, no doubt uncomfortable at the prospect of a monarchical executive. Benjamin Franklin broke the silence and asked for opinions on the subject.

John Rutledge spoke first. He was the most respected man in his State. He had been governor—and de facto commander-in-chief—of South Carolina during the war, and would later serve on the United States Supreme Court. Rutledge said "he was for vesting the executive power in a single person, though he was not for giving him the power of war and peace. A single man," he reasoned, "would feel the greatest responsibility, and administer the public affairs best." Roger Sherman responded that "he considered the executive magistracy as nothing more than an institution for carrying the will of the legislature into effect...."[3] James Wilson thought the Convention should avoid the "British monarch as a proper guide," and argued that the "only powers he considered strictly executive were those of executing the laws, and appointing officers." Edmund Randolph rejoined that he considered a single executive as "the foetus of monarchy." Wilson answered that "unity in the executive, instead of being the foetus of monarchy, would be the best safeguard against tyranny."[4]

With the exception of Alexander Hamilton, Wilson pushed harder for a single executive than any man in the Philadelphia Convention. He believed that "the people of Amer. did not oppose the British King but the parliament—the opposition was not agt. an Unity but a corrupt multitude." And he argued that the "extent" of the United States required "the vigour of Monarchy" while the "manners...are purely republican." His greatest concern was a "vigourous execution of the Laws."[5] He also remarked that "all know that a single magistrate is not a King..." and "all the 13 States, tho' agreeing in scarce any other instance, agree in placing a single magistrate at the head of the Government."[6] Wilson may have overstated his case in the first instance—the Declaration of Independence was in fact an indictment of the king, and the Articles of Confederation purposely eliminated an executive branch—but most agreed on his final point. Roger Sherman, however, noted that while Wilson was correct in his characterization of State executives, he also noted that each State had a "Council of advice, without which the first magistrate could not act." He thought this was the only way to make a single executive "acceptable to the people."[7] That was the crux of the argument against a single executive: unless the executive was subjected to some sort of oversight, he could easily abuse his power.

George Mason made this a central theme of his attack on the executive, both during the Convention, and once it wrapped up its business in September 1787. In June 1787, Mason remarked, "If strong and extensive Powers are vested in the Executive, and that Executive consists of only one Person; the Government will of course degenerate (for I will call it degeneracy) into a Monarchy—a Government so contrary to the Genius of the people that they will reject even the Appearance of it...." Plus, Mason contended a plural executive, which he initially advanced, elected from the three sections of the Union, would "bring...a more perfect and extensive Knowledge of the real Interests of this great Union" and would restrain and counteract "the aspiring Views of dangerous and ambitious Men."[8] In the absence of a plural executive, Mason argued a council of advice could provide similar safeguards.

Mason listed a lack of a council as one of the principle defects of the Constitution in his famous and widely circulated objections. Without a council, he surmised the president would be "unsupported by proper Information & Advice; and will generally be directed by Minions & Favorites—or He will become a Tool of the Senate—or a Council of State will grow out of the principle Officers of the great Departments; the worst & most dangerous of all Ingredients for such a Council, in a free Country...."[9] A council comprised of men from each section would provide the president with sufficient information and would act as a check on his authority. Mason considered this an essential safeguard for the people of the States.

Randolph, in calling a single executive "the foetus of monarchy" and Mason, in displaying fear over potential abuse by a single executive, echoed many of the fears of the founding generation. New York Governor George Clinton, writing as "Cato," said in November 1787, "Compare your past opinions and sentiments with the present proposed establishment, and you will find, that if you adopt it, that it will lead you into a system which you heretofore reprobated as odious. Every American whig, not long since, bore his emphatic testimony against a monarchical government, though limited, because of the dangerous inequality that it created among citizens as relative to their rights and property; and wherein does this president, invested with his powers and prerogatives, essentially differ from the king of Great-Britain...."[10]

"An Old Whig" urged his readers to reconsider the Constitution if for no other reason than it created an elected king. "If we are not prepared to *receive a king,* let us call another convention to revise the proposed constitution, and form it anew on the principles of [a] confederacy of free republics; but by no means, under pretence of a republic, to lay the foundation for a military government, which is the worst of all tyrannies."[11]

These were popular opinions, and they forced the opposition to work hard during the months leading to ratification to persuade the people of the States that their liberty would be safe under such a system. During the Pennsylvania Ratifying Convention, James Wilson argued that a single executive furnishes security. "The executive power is better to be trusted when it has no screen"—that is, every move of a single executive would be watched and scrutinized. "He cannot act improperly, and hide either his negligence or inattention; he cannot roll upon any other person the weight of his criminality...and he is responsible for every nomination he makes." Most important, Wilson argued that a single executive provided "vigor," a word he championed quite often during the Philadelphia Convention.[12]

Hamilton focused on the executive in several of the Federalist essays. In Federalist No. 70, he famously wrote, "There can be no need however to multiply arguments or examples on this head. A feeble executive implies a feeble execution of the government.

A feeble execution is but another phrase for a bad execution: And a government ill executed, whatever it may be in theory, must be in practice a bad government." Like Wilson, Hamilton insisted that vigor required "unity." "Decision, activity, secrecy, and dispatch will generally characterise the proceedings of one man, in a much more eminent degree, than the proceedings of any greater number; and in proportion as the number is increased, these qualities will be diminished."[13] Of course, in March 1788, when this essay appeared in the New York press, the public was unaware that Hamilton had advanced a plan in the Philadelphia Convention which would have essentially created a king of the United States.[14] He scoffed at those who argued the Constitution would do that, but privately wished for such a result. It must be said that of all the public advocates for the ratification of the Constitution, Hamilton was the most skilled with the pen but also the most disingenuous.

William Richardson Davie provided the best summary explanation of the single executive during the First North Carolina Ratifying Convention. He said, "With respect to the unity of the executive, the superior energy and secrecy wherewith one person can act, was one of the principles on which the Convention went. But a more predominant principle was, the more obvious responsibility of one person. It was observed that, if there were a plurality of persons, and a crime should be committed, when their conduct came to be examined, it would be impossible to fix the fact on any one of them."[15] The founding generation generally considered a single executive to be the best and most efficient means of enforcing the laws of the Union, and the most secure way of ensuring transparency and accountability in the executive branch. Yet, perhaps George Mason was the most perceptive when he opined that the executive would be controlled by his "Minions & Favorites."

And, while not a king, each successive president has over time arrogated tremendous power to the executive branch. That was not supposed to happen under the Constitution *as ratified*.

Many of the arguments against a single executive were tied to the length of time the president would hold office. Initial proposals ranged from three years to seven years, with Hamilton advocating a lifetime appointment. The final draft establishing a four year term with the prospect of re-election was a compromise between the two competing camps: those who thought the executive should continually rotate and those who believed the executive should remain in office for as long as the people would permit.

The Philadelphia Convention agreed to the prospect of re-eligibility in July 1787. Roger Sherman had remarked earlier in the Convention that removing the prospect of re-election would potentially prevent good men from holding office. Gouverneur Morris said in July that "ineligibility...tended to destroy the great motive to good behavior, the hope of being rewarded by a re-appointment."[16] The pressing problem, however, was the coupling of re-eligibility with a lengthy term of seven years. Several members of the Convention raised a red flag over such a prospect. James McClurg of Virginia moved to replace a seven-year term with the phrase "during good behavior." This found favor among Gouverneur Morris and Jacob Broom of Delaware, but Sherman argued that such a statement was unnecessary. "As the Executive Magistrate is now re-eligible, he will be on good behavior as far as will be necessary. If he behaves well he will be continued; if otherwise, displaced on a succeeding election." George Mason said such an arrangement was "a softer name only for an Executive for life. And that the next would be an easy step to hereditary Monarchy."[17]

Madison replied that a strong executive would *prevent* monarchy by restraining the powers of the legislature. In a short speech, he outlined what would later be called the "checks and balances" of the government. Madison argued that the executive should be independent of both the legislature and the judicial branch, and only by checking the ability of the legislature to encroach on the executive through long term lengths would the prospect of "revolution" be avoided.

James McClurg clarified his recommendation "of good behavior" as setting the term of office by stating that "it was an essential object with him to make the Executive independent of the Legislature; and the only mode left for effecting it…was to appoint him during good behavior."[18] Madison noted in his journal that only three or four members of the Convention supported a term "during good behavior," and that their adherence to this principle was tenuous. The delegates did not want a king, but an independent executive free from abuse by the other branches of government.

The Convention debated term length and limits for several days in July, with Gouverneur Morris and Edmund Randolph taking the lead in the verbal sparring. Morris insisted that the only way to preserve an independent executive was "either to give him his office for life, or make him eligible [electable] by the people."[19] Randolph responded that if the executive wished to remain independent, "he should not be left under a temptation to court a re-appointment." Randolph saw re-eligibility as the problem, not term length. "It has been said that a constitutional bar to reappointment will inspire unconstitutional endeavours to perpetuate himself. It may be answered that his endeavours can have no effect unless the people be corrupt to such a degree as to render all precautions hopeless: to which may be added that this argument supposes him to be more powerful & dangerous, than other arguments which have been used, admit, and consequently calls for stronger fetters on his authority."[20] When the smoke cleared in mid-July, the Convention determined that the executive would be eligible for re-election with a six-year term. The shift occurred when the method of election was changed from the general legislature to the Electoral College system (which will be discussed later), but this did not end the debate.

As with other provisions in the Constitution, opponents kept pressing the issue even after it appeared resolved. When the Convention reversed course and replaced the Electoral College system again at the end of July, proposals for ten-, fifteen-, and even twenty-year terms were floated in order to mock the very idea of a long-term executive appointment. Rufus King quipped that twenty years was the "medium life of princes" in the hope that such an outrageous term would thwart a move away from the Electoral College.[21] It worked, but the see-saw battle over the method of electing the executive continued until almost the final day. In the end, the Committee of Detail settled on a four-year term with the president eligible for re-election. By September, the delegates were simply eager for a resolution and quickly agreed. Only North Carolina dissented.

When the Constitution was sent to the States for ratification, the re-eligibility of the president was seized upon by opponents to show that the Constitution would create a monarchy on the ruins of the federal republic. Luther Martin, who had attempted on several occasions during the Philadelphia Convention to make the president ineligible for a second term, questioned, "What state in the union considers it advantageous to its interest, that the President should be re-eligible…?"[22] In his famous open letter on the

Constitution, Edmund Randolph urged the people of Virginia to insist on "rendering the President ineligible after a given number of years...."[23] And the "Centinel" thought that the construction of the executive branch, in conjunction with other questionable powers in the government, would make the government "in practice a *permanent* ARISTOCRACY."[24]

George Mason, in the Virginia Ratifying Convention, remarked:

> Mr. Chairman, there is not a more important article in the Constitution than this. The great fundamental principle of responsibility in republicanism is here sapped. The President is elected without rotation. It may be said that a new election may remove him, and place another in his stead. If we judge from the experience of all other countries, and even our own, we may conclude that, as the President of the United States may be reëlected, so he will. How is it in every government where rotation is not required? Is there a single instance of a great man not being reëlected? Our governor is obliged to return, after a given period, to a private station. It is so in most of the states. This President will be elected time after time: he will be continued in office for life. If we wish to change him, the great powers in Europe will not allow us.[25]

Proponents of the Constitution were quick to parry. Roger Sherman suggested the four-year term and the option of re-eligibility would provide "great security for...fidelity in office, and will give greater stability and energy to government than an exclusion by rotation, and will be an operative and effectual security against arbitrary government, either monarchical or aristocratic."[26] Hamilton, in Federalist No. 72, wrote that re-eligibility was "necessary to give to the officer himself the inclination and the resolution to act his part well, and to the community time and leisure to observe the tendency of his measures, and thence to form an experimental estimate of their merits . . . [and] when they see reason to approve of his conduct, to continue him in the station, in order to prolong the utility of his talents and virtues, and to secure to the government, the advantage of permanency in a wise system of administration."[27]

Archibald Maclaine of North Carolina, in attempting to prove that the president would neither be a king nor comparable to the monarchs of Europe, summarized what the founding generation feared most from executive authority when he defended the executive in March 1788:

> The enemies of the new form of government endeavour to persuade others, what I can scarcely think they believe themselves; that, the President of the United States is only another name for King, and that we shall be subject to all the evils of a monarchical government. How a magistrate, who is removeable at a short period, can be compared to an hereditary monarch, whose family, to all succeeding generations, as well as himself must be maintained in pomp and splendour, at an enormous expence to the nation; and whose power and influence will be proportionably great, these honest guardians of the rights of the people would do well to inform us. . . ."[28]

Reading his comments with the modern American "imperial presidency" in mind only illustrates how far the United States has
strayed from the original intent of the Constitution.

Ultimately, proponents of the Constitution believed that the
potential power of impeachment would temper executive abuse.
Maclaine suggested as much when he reiterated that the "President
of the United States will be liable to be impeached by the
representatives of the people, and to be tried for his crimes" should
they occur.[29] The Framers designed the executive branch with this
power in mind, and from the earliest debates in Philadelphia, the
ability to impeach the president was considered essential to
preserving republican government.

John Dickinson thought "it was necessary...to place the power
to remove somewhere," though he was not certain which branch
should have control.[30] William Richardson Davie thought if the
president was not impeachable, "he will spare no efforts or means
whatever to get himself re-elected" and he "considered this as an
essential security for the good behaviour of the Executive."[31] George
Mason said, "No point is of more importance than that the right
of impeachment should be continued. Shall any man be above
Justice? Above all shall that man be above it, who can commit the
most extensive injustice?" Benjamin Franklin thought the power
of impeachment would not only preserve republican government,
but would be "favorable to the executive." "It would be the best way
therefore to provide in the Constitution for the regular punishment
of the Executive when his misconduct should deserve it, and for
his honorable acquittal when he should be unjustly accused."[32] And
Elbridge Gerry, in plain spoken fashion, said, "A good magistrate
will not fear them [impeachments]. A bad one ought to be kept in

fear of them. He hoped the maxim would never be adopted here that the chief Magistrate could do (no) wrong."[33]

Charles Pinckney had the most interesting argument against the power of impeachment. He believed impeachment would be unnecessary because "his [the president's] powers would be so circumscribed" by the Constitution. In other words, he did not fear executive abuse because there would be little power delegated to that branch, and he questioned why other members of the Philadelphia Convention "reasoned on a supposition that the Executive was to have powers which would not be committed to him...."[34] Pinckney was right that little power would be *constitutionally* delegated to the president, but he was naïve to think that ambitious men would not attempt to expand those powers *unconstitutionally*. The rest of the delegates were trying to check that potential through the threat of impeachment, and, as it turns out, rightly so.

After the Constitution was presented to the States for ratification, proponents trumpeted the power of impeachment as a way to persuade wavering individuals that the president could never abuse his power. Writing as "Fabius" in April 1788, John Dickinson claimed that "this president will be no *dictator* [because] he is *removable* and *punishable* for misbehaviour."[35] Alexander Hamilton concluded his extensive defense of the executive in the Federalist by stating that the president could not abuse his authority because he was "at all times liable to impeachment."[36] Alexander Contee Hanson of Maryland—a judge who had been a private secretary to George Washington—wrote in 1788 that the president should not be feared because, "like any other individual, he is liable to punishment."[37] Writing as "Marcus," James Iredell argued, "The probability of the President of the United States committing an act of treason against his country is very slight; he is so well guarded by the other powers of government…that in my opinion it is the most chimerical apprehension that can be entertained. Such a thing is however possible, and accordingly he is not exempt from trial, if he should be guilty, or supposed guilty, of that or any other offense."[38] This was the general line of reasoning. Proponents believed impeachment provided enough security against executive abuse that the general public had nothing to fear from the new government. Yet not every opponent of the document was persuaded.

Luther Martin spoke for the majority of the opponents of the Constitution when he wrote in 1788 that "there is little reason to believe that a majority will ever concur in impeaching the president." The president, he believed, would have undue influence over the legislature due to his appointment powers. Additionally, Martin argued that the Senate could not be relied upon to convict the president if impeached. "The senate being constituted a privy council to the president, it is probable many of its leading and influential members may have advised and concurred in the very measures for which he may be impeached…." With this in mind, Martin could not fathom an occasion when the president would not have at least one-third of the Senate to support him, and thus he would never be found guilty.[39] Martin was prophetic. Only two presidents have been impeached and neither was convicted, though not because of the reasons he stated. The real issue, of course, is the vague phrase "Treason, Bribery, or other high Crimes and Misdemeanors." What did the founding generation think constituted an impeachable offense?

During the Philadelphia Convention, James Madison listed "incapacity," "negligence," "perfidy," "peculation," "oppression," and betraying "his trust to foreign powers" as the chief causes for impeachment. Edmund Randolph thought that the "Executive will have great opportunitys of abusing his power; particularly in time of war when the military force, and in some respects the public money will be in his hands." Gouverneur Morris thought "bribery," "treachery," and corruption were sufficient grounds for impeachment.[40] And during the Virginia Ratifying Convention, Madison called acts of a purely partisan nature a "misdemeanor."[41] Of course, the phrase "good behavior" was bandied about quite often during the ratification debates. The founding generation believed that meant the president should not abuse his trust or his power and should remain faithful to prescribed constitutional limits. Thus, "Perfidy" and "negligence" could be considered "high Crimes and Misdemeanors," as could abuse of power, and without question the founding generation believed that if the president broke the law he should be removed from office. Under this definition—if we adhered to the Constitution *as ratified* by the founding generation—several presidents in the last one hundred years should have been impeached and convicted for exceeding their constitutional authority, an abuse of power.

Executive Powers

"The President shall be Commander in Chief of the Army and Navy of the United States, and of the Militia of the several States, when called into the actual Service of the United States; he may require the Opinion, in writing, of the principal Officer in each of the executive Departments, upon any subject relating to the Duties of their respective Offices, and he shall have Power to

Grant Reprieves and Pardons for Offenses against the United States, except in Cases of Impeachment.

"He shall have Power, by and with the Advice and Consent of the Senate, to make Treaties, provided two thirds of the Senators present concur; and he shall nominate, and by and with the Advice and Consent of the Senate, shall appoint Ambassadors, other public Ministers and Consuls, Judges of the supreme Court, and all other Officers of the United States, whose Appointments are not herein otherwise provided for, and which shall be established by Law: but the Congress may by Law vest the Appointment of such inferior Officers, as they think proper, in the President alone, in the Courts of Law, or in the Heads of Departments.

"The President shall have Power to fill up all Vacancies that may happen during the Recess of the Senate, by granting Commissions which shall expire at the End of their next Session." **Article II, Section 2.**

"He shall from time to time give to the Congress Information of the State of the Union, and recommend to their Consideration such Measures as he shall judge necessary and expedient; he may, on extraordinary Occasions, convene both Houses, or either of them, and in Case of Disagreement between them, with Respect to the Time of Adjournment, he may adjourn them to such Time as he shall think proper; he shall receive Ambassadors and other public Ministers; he shall take Care that the Laws be faithfully executed, and shall Commission all the Officers of the United States."
Article II, Section 3.

"Every Bill which shall have passed the House of Representatives and the Senate, shall, before it become a Law, be presented to the President of the United States; If he approve he shall sign it, but if not he shall return it, with his Objections to that House in which it shall have originated, who shall enter the Objections at large on their Journal, and proceed to reconsider it. If after such Reconsideration two thirds of that House shall agree to pass the Bill, it shall be sent, together with the Objections, to the other House, by which it shall likewise be reconsidered, and if approved by two thirds of that House, it shall become a Law. But in all such Cases the Votes of both Houses shall be determined by Yeas and Nays, and the Names of the Persons voting for and against the Bill shall be entered on the Journal of each House respectively. If any Bill shall not be returned by the President within ten Days (Sundays excepted) after it shall have been presented to him, the Same shall be a Law, in like Manner as if he had signed it, unless the Congress by their Adjournment prevent its Return, in which Case it shall not be a Law." **Article I, Section 7, Clause 2.**

The executive powers contained in Article II are the most misrepresented component of the Constitution. You might expect to see a long list of delegated authority, but by design, there is little there. Congress has more constitutional power than the president, yet most Americans—including presidential candidates—mistakenly believe that the president controls taxes, spending, and a host of other domestic items. For example, during the 2008 presidential campaign, Barack Obama said, "Even if we're still in a recession,

I'm going to go through with my tax cuts."[42] And just two days after the November 2008 election, Jake Fox, writing for *Time* magazine said, "Let's be clear about this: Barack Obama isn't going to raise your taxes in 2009."[43] And who can forget George H. W. Bush's 1988 campaign pledge of, "Read my lips, no new taxes!" or the fact that the tax cuts of 2001 and 2003 are called the "Bush tax cuts." Bush did not cut taxes, Obama cannot raise or lower taxes, and George H. W. Bush's campaign pledge was simply a political ploy to get elected. Mr. Fox was right; Obama can never raise taxes, only Congress can. A president can certainly block legislation via the veto power, but even that power is not absolute. Understanding how the founding generation viewed executive authority when the Constitution was *ratified* would do much to correct public misconceptions about executive authority and perhaps return it to its proper place.

When executive authority was first discussed in the Philadelphia Convention, Roger Sherman suggested that the executive branch was "nothing more than an institution for carrying the will of the legislature into effect." In other words, Sherman did not believe the president should have legislative authority. His job should be to execute the laws and nothing more. James Wilson agreed, and argued that the British monarch was not "a proper guide in defining the executive powers. Some of these prerogatives were of a legislative nature; among others, that of war and peace, &c. The only powers he considered strictly executive were those of executing the laws, and appointing officers, not appertaining to, and appointed by, the legislature." James Madison responded that before they decided on a single or plural executive, the Convention should "fix the extent of the executive authority." He then proposed, with the advice of Charles Pinckney, that the president should have "power to carry into effect the national laws, to appoint to offices in cases not otherwise provided for, and to execute such other powers 'not legislative nor judiciary in their nature' as may from time to time be delegated by the national legislature."[44] The key point, of course, was the phrase "not legislative nor judiciary in nature." The Framers did not consider the president to be the chief legislator. He could not propose legislation and his primary domestic responsibility was to execute the laws and carry "the will of the legislature into effect."

By Article II, Section 2, the president is commander in chief of the United States military and head of state with treaty making authority and appointment powers. But even these powers are circumscribed by both Congress and the States. Congress declares war and appropriates money for the military. The president simply executes its will. The Senate, meaning the States, must concur on both executive appointments and treaties with foreign nations. According to the Constitution *as ratified*, the States and the people limited executive authority through the general legislature.

One of the greatest fears of the founding generation was an executive with unrestrained power over the sword. Charles Pinckney expressed alarm early in the Convention that the "executive powers…might extend to peace and war, &c."[45] Both his plan for a new Constitution and William Paterson's New Jersey Plan called for the executive to be the commander in chief, but Paterson's plan prohibited any of the executives (he advocated a plural executive) from personally taking command of the army. This, he hoped, would quell the potential of a military dictator.

Opponents of the Constitution, such as Luther Martin, echoed the restrictions set forth in the New Jersey Plan.[46] Others, such as Gilbert Livingston of New York, advocated a constitutional amendment that would have prohibited the president from commanding the military in person without the consent of Congress.[47]

Robert Miller of North Carolina argued that the president's "influence would be too great in the country, and particularly over the military, by being commander-in-chief of the army, navy, and militia. He thought he could too easily abuse such extensive powers...."[48] George Mason, in the Virginia Ratifying Convention, spoke for the majority who opposed executive war powers when he said he "admitted the propriety of his [the president] being commander-in-chief, so far as to give orders and have a general superintendency, but he thought it would be dangerous to let him command in person, without any restraint, as he might make a bad use of it." Mason, like Livingston and Miller, thought Congress should be required to authorize personal command of the military, for "so disinterested and amiable a character as General Washington might never command again."[49] Mason accepted the president's role of commander in chief within the limits prescribed by the Constitution but wanted safeguards against the possibility of a military dictatorship.

James Iredell argued that the president's power as commander in chief was already "sufficiently guarded."

> A very material difference may be observed between this power, and the authority of the king of Great Britain under similar circumstances. The king of Great Britain is not only the commander-in-chief of the land and naval forces, but has power, in time of war, to raise fleets and armies. He has also authority to declare war. *The President has not the power of declaring war by his own authority, nor that of raising fleets and armies* [emphasis added]. These powers are vested in other hands. The power of declaring war is expressly given to

Congress, that is, to the two branches of the legislature—the Senate, composed of representatives of the
state legislatures, the House of Representatives, deputed
by the people at large. They have also expressly delegated to them the powers of raising and supporting
armies, and of providing and maintaining a navy.

With regard to the militia, it must be observed, that
though he has the command of them when called into
the actual service of the United States, yet he has not the
power of calling them out. The power of calling them
out is vested in Congress, for the purpose of executing
the laws of the Union. When the militia are called out
for any purpose, some person must command them;
and who so proper as that person who has the best
evidence of his possessing the general confidence of the
people? I trust, therefore, that the power of commanding the militia, when called forth into the actual service
of the United States, will not be objected to.[50]

George Nicholas of Virginia followed a similar argument. "The
army and navy were to be raised by Congress, and not by the
President.... As to possible danger, any commander might attempt
to pervert what was intended for the common defense of the community to its destruction. The President, at the end of four years,
was to relinquish all his offices. But if any other person was to have
the command, the time would not be limited."[51]

Hamilton, in typical condescending fashion, summarily dismissed any arguments against the president's role as commander
in chief in Federalist No. 74. "The President of the United States is
to be 'Commander in Chief of the army and navy of the United

States, and of the militia of the several States *when called into the actual service* of the United States.' The propriety of this provision is so evident in itself; and it is at the same time so consonant to the precedents of the State constitutions in general, that little need be said to explain or enforce it."[52] George Mason did not believe "that the propriety of this provision" was "so evident." "The liberty of the people had been destroyed by those who were military commanders only. The danger here was greater by the junction of great civil powers to the command of the army and fleet. Although Congress are to raise the army, said he, no security arises from that; for, in time of war, they must and ought to raise an army, which will be numerous, or otherwise, according to the nature of the war, and then the President is to command without any control."[53]

This is one area, however, where proponents have been generally vindicated. Only two presidents have personally commanded the military, George Washington and James Madison. The real threat to constitutional war powers was not personal leadership by the executive, but the passage of the War Powers Resolution in 1973. This authorized the president to send the military into action abroad without immediate congressional approval. It clearly violated the Constitution *as ratified*—and then-President Richard Nixon actually tried to veto it, but was overridden—and enlarged executive powers beyond those the founding generation were comfortable vesting in the president. Though some of the Framers thought the president should be able to "repel sudden attacks," that by no means encompassed the broad powers granted by the War Powers Resolution. As Iredell said, the president cannot call out the army and navy. The term "commander-in-chief" only applied to the president when the army was constitutionally called into service.

Critics of this position will point to the Quasi-War with France during the John Adams administration, or the action taken by Thomas Jefferson in dealing with the Barbary Pirates from 1801 to 1805 as justification for broad executive authority over war. But there are differences between the actions taken by these administrations and those taken by Lyndon B. Johnson or George W. Bush. To be sure, both Adams and Jefferson, with congressional authorization, instructed the United States Navy to protect American shipping and destroy enemy privateers and warships, but in contrast to the Vietnam War or the invasion of Iraq in 2003, the United States Navy was not "making" war; it was defending American sovereignty, neutrality, and commerce, and the president was fulfilling his duty as commander in chief of the navy.

Presidential appointment and treaty-making powers also came under attack during the ratification debates. When the former issue was discussed during the Philadelphia Convention, there was disagreement over which branch of government should be vested with the power of appointment. John Rutledge thought that giving it to the executive would make "the people think we are leaning too much towards Monarchy." Madison preferred the Senate because of its stability and independence.[54] Nathaniel Gorham suggested giving States a check against executive power by stipulating that the executive should make appointments with the advice and consent of the Senate. As Luther Martin pointed out during the same debate, the Senate was chosen "from all the States [and] would be best informed of characters & most capable of making a fit choice."[55] Madison agreed that having executive appointments approved by the Senate "would unite the advantage of responsibility in the Executive with the security afforded in the second branch against any incautious or corrupt nomination by the Executive."[56] Madison's version of "advice and consent" ultimately found its way into the text of the Constitution.

As for the power to make treaties with foreign powers, original drafts of the Constitution vested this power exclusively in the Senate. Madison demurred, saying, "that the Senate represented the States alone, and that for this as well as other obvious reasons it was proper that the President should be an agent in Treaties."[57] As with the power of appointments, a compromise was reached where treaties would be binding only after they were approved not only by the president, but by a two-thirds majority in the Senate.

In the case of both executive appointments and treaty-making authority, critics charged that requiring a two-thirds majority in the Senate would allow the minority to hijack the process and, moreover, that it mixed executive and legislative powers, which should be kept separate. George Mason remarked that "five states may make a treaty; ten senators—the representatives of five states—being two thirds of a quorum. These ten might come from the smallest states.... His principal fear, however, was not that five, but that seven, states—a bare majority—would make treaties to bind the Union."[58] Samuel Spencer, in the First North Carolina Ratifying Convention, argued that "the combining in the Senate the power of legislation, with a controlling share in the appointment of all the officers of the United States, (except those chosen by the people,)...invests the Senate at once with such an enormity of power, and with such an overbearing and uncontrollable influence, as is incompatible with every idea of safety to the liberties of a free country, and is calculated to swallow up all other powers, and to render that body a despotic aristocracy."[59] "Brutus" called the Senate a "strange mixture of legislative, executive, and judicial powers," particularly in reference to their powers under Article II, Section 2.[60]

Both James Iredell and William Richardson Davie were masterful in their responses in the First North Carolina Ratifying Convention. Davie stated that "the power of making treaties has, in all countries and governments, been placed in the executive departments." But he also reserved a role for the Senate, because it was important that a majority of the States affirmed their support of treaties.[61] Iredell seconded, defending the importance of having the Senate ratify treaties: "for in this case the sovereignty of the states is particularly concerned, and the great caution of giving the states an equality of suffrage in making treaties, was for the express purpose of taking care of that sovereignty, and attending to their interests, as political bodies, in foreign negotiations."[62]

In Virginia, George Nicholas, in response to George Mason, argued that, "The possibility of five states making treaties was founded on a supposition of the non-attendance of the senators from the other states. This non-attendance, he observed, might be reciprocated. It was presumable that, on such important occasions, they would attend from all the states, and then there must be a concurrence of nine states. The approbation of the President, who had no local views, being elected by no particular state, but the people at large, was an additional security."[63] Ultimately it was Francis Corbin of Virginia who had the best defense of the clause:

> If, says he, there be any sound part in this Constitution, it is in this clause. The representatives are excluded from interposing in making treaties, because large popular assemblies are very improper to transact such business, from the impossibility of their acting with sufficient secrecy, despatch, and decision, which can only be found in small bodies, and because such

numerous bodies are ever subject to factions and party animosities. *It would be dangerous to give this power to the President alone, as the concession of such power to one individual is repugnant to republican principles.* It is, therefore, given to the President and the Senate (who represent the states in their individual capacities) conjointly. In this it differs from every government we know. It steers with admirable dexterity between the two extremes, neither leaving it to the executive, as in most other governments, nor to the legislative, which would too much retard such negotiation.[64] (emphasis added)

In the modern era, presidents have often resorted to so-called executive agreements—made between the president and a foreign power, and not requiring congressional approval—as a way to circumvent the treaty process. Supporters of executive agreements often point to Thomas Jefferson as the progenitor of the practice. But both Jefferson and Madison thought the legislature, including the House of Representatives, should have a role in foreign policy. Madison, in fact, fought strenuously against George Washington's Neutrality Proclamation in 1793 on the basis that only Congress could make such a rule. It is true that Jefferson defended what are often called "congressional-executive agreements" while Secretary of State, but these, as their name implies, were not unilateral executive agreements, and they were limited to commercial treaties.[65]

Such "congressional-executive agreements" were defended and explained by Richard Henry Lee, a limited-government opponent of the Constitution, in *The Federal Farmer* in 1788:

On a fair construction of the constitution, I think the
legislature has a proper controul over the president and
senate in settling commercial treaties. By art. 1. sect. 2.
the legislature will have power to regulate commerce
with foreign nations, &c. By art. 2. sect. 2. the president,
with the advice and consent of two-thirds of the senate,
may make treaties. These clauses must be considered
together, and we ought never to make one part of the
same instrument contradict another, if it can be
avoided by any reasonable construction. By the first
recited clause, the legislature has the power, that is, as I
understand it, the sole power to regulate commerce
with foreign nations, or to make all the rules and
regulations respecting trade and commerce between
our citizens and foreigners: by the second recited clause,
the president and senate have power generally to make
treaties.—There are several kinds of treaties—as
treaties of commerce, of peace, of alliance, &c. I think
the words to "make treaties," may be consistently
construed, and yet so as it shall be left to the legislature
to confirm commercial treaties; they are in their nature
and operation very distinct from treaties of peace and
of alliance; the latter generally require secrecy, it is but
very seldom they interfere with the laws and internal
police of the country; to make them is properly the
exercise of executive powers, and the constitution
authorises the president and senate to make treaties,
and gives the legislature no power, directly or indirectly,
respecting these treaties of peace and alliance. As to
treaties of commerce, they do not generally require

secrecy, they almost always involve in them legislative powers, interfere with the laws and internal police of the country, and operate immediately on persons and property, especially in the commercial towns: (they have in Great-Britain usually been confirmed by parliament;) they consist of rules and regulations respecting commerce; and to regulate commerce, or to make regulations respecting commerce, the federal legislature, by the constitution, has the power. I do not see that any commercial regulations can be made in treaties, that will not infringe upon this power in the legislature: therefore, I infer, that the true construction is, that the president and senate shall make treaties; but all commercial treaties shall be subject to be confirmed by the legislature. This construction will render the clauses consistent, and make the powers of the president and senate, respecting treaties, much less exceptionable.[66]

While Lee, Jefferson, and Madison defended so-called congressional-executive agreements in relation to commerce *alone*, no member of the founding generation supported unilateral executive agreements, which they would have regarded as monarchical and dangerous to liberty. Even Washington, during the height of a showdown with the Senate over an unpopular treaty with Great Britain, placed a negotiated treaty on their desks for their approval or rejection. Most modern presidents have not given the Senate that luxury. In fact, since 1939, close to 95 percent of all foreign agreements have been unilateral executive agreements, including some controversial decisions, such as United States involvement in the World Bank, the IMF, G.A.T.T., and N.A.F.T.A. According to the Constitution *as ratified*, the Senate, as the agent of the States, was a strong check on the power of the executive branch. That is how proponents sold executive powers to the State Ratifying Conventions. The executive was never to have unbridled authority over appointments or foreign policy. That is how the majority of the founding generation interpreted Article II, Section 2.

Veto Power

The word "veto" is Latin for "I forbid." Articulated in Article I, Section 7, Clause 2, the presidential authority to veto laws is an important component of the executive powers and received considerable attention both during the Philadelphia Convention and in the months leading to ratification. The veto power is also often misunderstood. The first five presidents—all members of the founding generation—issued a total of ten vetoes. Neither John Adams nor Thomas Jefferson issued even one. The founding generation considered the veto power a measure of last resort against unconstitutional legislation passed by Congress. It was not designed as a way for the president to thwart legislation he didn't like. As per Article II, Section 3, the president is charged with executing the laws Congress passes as long as they are constitutional. The president is not the chief legislator or a prime minister, at least not according to the Constitution *as ratified*.

James Wilson first proposed that the executive have "an absolute negative" during the Philadelphia Convention. He argued that without this power, "the Legislature can at any moment sink it into non-existence."[67] And he then explained that he thought the "power would be seldom used. The Legislature would know that such a power existed, and would refrain from such laws, as it would be sure to defeat. Its silent operation would therefore preserve harmony and prevent mischief." Wilson, however, was pressing a lost cause.

Opponents immediately rebelled against this idea. Elbridge Gerry saw "no necessity for so great a controul over the legislature as the best men in the Community would be comprised in the two branches of it." Benjamin Franklin feared that "if a negative should be given as proposed, that more power and money would be demanded, till at last eno' would be gotten to influence & bribe the Legislature into a compleat subjection to the will of the Executive." Roger Sherman was more direct. "No one man could be found so far above the rest in wisdom." The executive, he suggested, could help revise the laws, but not "overrule the decided and cool opinions of the Legislature."[68] Pierce Butler said that "could he have entertained an idea that a compleat negative on the laws was to be given him he certainly should have acted differently [and voted against a single executive]. It had been observed that in all countries the Executive power is in a constant course of increase." Gunning Bedford of Delaware remarked that he opposed "every check on the Legislative.... He thought it would be sufficient to mark out in the Constitution the boundaries to the Legislative Authority, which would give all the requisite security to the rights of the other departments. The Representatives of the People were the best judges of what was for their interest, and ought to be under no external controul whatever."[69]

The final two speeches before a vote was taken on the issue conveyed the most apprehension over the potential for executive abuse. George Mason expressed dismay at the course of the Convention, particularly in regard to the creation of a singular executive with extensive powers. "We are not indeed constituting a British Government, but a more dangerous monarchy, an elective one.... He hoped that nothing like a monarchy would ever be attempted in this Country. A hatred to its oppressions had carried the people through the late Revolution." Franklin concluded his second speech on the issue with the following warning: "The first man, put at the helm will be a good one [George Washington]. No body knows what sort may come afterwards. The executive will be always increasing here, as elsewhere, till it ends in a monarchy."[70] All States voted against an absolute negative.

Both Gerry and James Madison came up with alternate proposals. The president would have a negative, but two-thirds of the congress could override his veto. Madison argued this would serve the same purpose as an absolute negative, but he thought the president would never "have firmness eno' to resist the Legislature unless backed by a certain part of the body itself [Madison crossed out 'or actuated by some foreign support agst. his own Country']." Gerry thought the veto was more of a "revisionary" procedure designed to protect against "unjust or unwise" legislation, and supported the two-thirds majority over-ride of the executive veto. This proposal passed by an 8 to 2 vote and was part of the final draft of the Constitution.[71]

Considering the attention it received during the Philadelphia Convention, it would have been shocking had the veto power not been examined during the ratification debates. William Findley was one of the first opponents of the Constitution to publicly attack the veto power after the Constitution was presented to the States for ratification. Findley, writing as "An Officer of the Late Continental Army," argued that in contrast to the "*nominal negative*" given to the king of England, the Constitution "intended" the president and the Senate to use the veto and "*support each other in the exercise of it.*"[72] He later charged in the Pennsylvania Ratifying

Convention that the veto power dangerously blended the executive with the legislative branch. "No bill can become law without [the president's] revision," Findley argued.[73]

Luther Martin, in *Genuine Information VI*, said, "And it was further urged, even if he was allowed a negative, it ought not to be of so great extent as that given by the system, since his *single voice* is to countervail the *whole* of *either* branch, and any number *less* than *two-thirds* of the other; however, a majority of the convention was of a different opinion, and adopted it as it now makes a part of the system." Moreover, Martin said, "That the *President* was not likely to have *more wisdom* or *integrity* than the *senators*, or *any of them*, or to *better know* or *consult* the interest of the States, than *any member* of the Senate, so as to be entitled to a negative on that principle." Because Congress included members from different States, Martin said that "there would always be a sufficient guard against measures being *hastily* or *rashly* adopted."[74]

William Lancaster, a delegate to the First North Carolina Ratifying Convention, said giving the president the power to veto laws allowed him to "overrule fifteen members of the Senate and every member of the House of Representatives." He considered such power "oppressive."[75] "The Impartial Examiner" of Virginia thought that the veto power placed the president on the doorstep of absolute monarchy. "If the system proposed had been calculated to extend his authority a little farther, he would preponderate against all—he alone would possess the sovereignty of America."[76]

Of course proponents of the Constitution did not see it that way. James Wilson directly refuted the charge linking the veto to "legislative authority." Speaking before the Pennsylvania Ratifying Convention, Wilson contended that "the [Philadelphia] Convention observed, on this occasion, strict propriety of language: 'If he approve the bill, when it is sent, he shall sign it, but if not, he shall return it;' but no bill passes in consequence of having his assent: therefore, he possesses no legislative authority. The *effect* of this power, upon this subject, is merely this: if he disapproved a bill, two thirds of the legislature become necessary to pass it into a law, instead of a bare majority. And when two thirds are in favor of the bill, it becomes a law, not by his, but by authority of the two houses of the legislature."[77] Wilson's statements are instructive for two reasons. First, he emphasized that, under the Constitution, the president would not be chief legislator or prime minister. Second, Wilson said the Constitution should be read in its "strict propriety of language." In short, there were no powers to be found "between the lines."

In Federalist No. 73, Alexander Hamilton remarked that the veto "not only serves as a shield to the executive, but it furnishes an additional security against the enaction of improper laws. It establishes a salutary check upon the legislative body calculated to guard the community against the effects of faction, precipitancy, or of any impulse unfriendly to the public good, which may happen to influence a majority of that body." Hamilton additionally echoed Wilson's remarks during the Philadelphia Convention about the "silent operation" of the veto power. "A power of this nature, in the executive, will often have a silent and unperceived though forcible operation. When men engaged in unjustifiable pursuits are aware, that obstructions may come from a quarter which they cannot controul, they will often be restrained, by the bare apprehension of opposition, from doing what they would with eagerness rush into, if no such external impediments were to be feared."[78]

James Iredell called the veto power a "happy medium between the possession of an absolute negative, and the executive having no control whatever on acts of legislation; and at the same time that it serves to protect the executive from ill designs in the legislature, it may also answer the purposes of preventing many laws passing which would be immediately injurious to the people at large. It is a strong guard against abuses in all, that the President's reasons are to be entered at large on the Journals, and, if the bill passes notwithstanding, that the yeas and nays are also to be entered. The public, therefore, can judge fairly between them."[79] The veto, then, was part of the system's checks and balances.

The men who followed the founding generation in office—particularly the "progressive presidents"—have found ways to circumvent the Constitution by issuing executive orders and "signing statements." The most egregious executive orders have carried the weight of law and in effect have acted as legislation. They are nothing short of presidential decrees and if the founding generation considered this a possibility, the Constitution never would have been ratified. Signing statements are similar to executive orders, except they accompany legislation and are an attempt by the executive branch to either reject or enlarge portions of a bill. Both violate the fundamental principle of maintaining a separation of powers—something the Founders believed was essential for free government.[80]

The Electoral College

"Each State shall appoint, in such Manner as the Legislature thereof may direct, a Number of Electors, equal to the whole Number of Senators and Representatives to which the State may be entitled in the Congress: but no Senator or Representative, or Person holding an

Office of Trust or Profit under the United States, shall be appointed an Elector." **Article II, Section 1, Clause 2.**

"The Electors shall meet in their respective states, and vote by ballot for President and Vice-President, one of whom, at least, shall not be an inhabitant of the same state with themselves; they shall name in their ballots the person voted for as President, and in distinct ballots the person voted for as Vice-President, and they shall make distinct lists of all persons voted for as President, and of all persons voted for as Vice-President and of the number of votes for each, which lists they shall sign and certify, and transmit sealed to the seat of the government of the United States, directed to the President of the Senate;

"The President of the Senate shall, in the presence of the Senate and House of Representatives, open all the certificates and the votes shall then be counted;

"The person having the greatest Number of votes for President, shall be the President, if such number be a majority of the whole number of Electors appointed; and if no person have such majority, then from the persons having the highest numbers not exceeding three on the list of those voted for as President, the House of Representatives shall choose immediately, by ballot, the President. But in choosing the President, the votes shall be taken by states, the representation from each state having one vote; a quorum for this purpose shall consist of a member or members from two-thirds of the states, and a majority of all the states shall be necessary to a choice. And if the House of Representatives shall not choose a President whenever the right of choice shall devolve upon them, before the fourth day of March next following, then the Vice-President shall act as President, as in the case of the death or other constitutional disability of the President.

"The person having the greatest number of votes as Vice-President, shall be the Vice-President, if such number be a majority of the whole number of Electors appointed, and if no person have a majority, then from the two highest numbers on the list, the Senate shall choose the Vice-President; a quorum for the purpose shall consist of two-thirds of the whole number of Senators, and a majority of the whole number shall be necessary to a choice. But no person constitutionally ineligible to the office of President shall be eligible to that of Vice-President of the United States."
Amendment XII.

The Electoral College is one of the most complex and controversial provisions of the Constitution. Various proposals to eliminate or reform the system have circulated for years, with the most successful being the National Popular Vote Bill. As of 2011, thirty-one States have passed the Bill with seven States having enacted the legislation. The idea is simple: each State that enacts the Bill pledges their Electoral votes to the candidate who won the total popular vote regardless of the vote total in that State. Thus, a candidate could theoretically lose a State and still control that State's Electoral votes. If adopted by all fifty States and the District of Columbia, it would ensure a unanimous victory in the Electoral

College. Supporters of the National Popular Vote movement argue that while the Bill reforms the Electoral College it does not destroy it. Regardless, they say, the system has been broken for years, and presidential elections are already popularity contests, why not make it official? Their marketing ploy is slick and ingenious, and they partly get the original intent of the Electoral College correct, but this type of legislation undermines what the founding generation intended the Electoral College to accomplish.

Delegates to the Philadelphia Convention debated several methods of electing the president. Madison's Virginia Plan had the legislature choosing the executive, and this was the most popular method for most of the Convention. Several members of the Convention made clear why they supported this mode of election. Roger Sherman "thought that the sense of the Nation would be better expressed by the Legislature, than by the people at large. The latter will never be sufficiently informed of characters. ..." Charles Pinckney said, "An Election by the people being liable to the most obvious & striking objections. They will be led by a few active & designing men." And George Mason argued that "it would be as unnatural to refer the choice of a proper character for chief Magistrate to the people, as it would, to refer a trial of colours to a blind man. The extent of the Country renders it impossible that the people can have the requisite capacity to judge of the respective pretensions of the Candidates."[81]

Two members of the Convention, James Wilson and Gouverneur Morris, consistently supported the election of the president by the people at large, but this was generally rejected as impractical and dangerous. Pierce Butler suggested that such a method would "disgust the States."[82] The plan finally adopted in July, proposed by Oliver Ellsworth, called for Electors from each State to choose the president. These Electors would be selected by the State legislatures. This was viewed as the ideal compromise. The people would choose their State representatives and then the States would, essentially, choose the president. The States are the critical element in the Electoral College. That is how the institution should be viewed, as an agent of the will of the people of the States. When Wilson initially proposed to strip the States of a role in the process by having the people at large elect the president, Elbridge Gerry responded that "it would alarm & give a handle to the State partizans, as tending to supersede altogether the State authorities. He thought the Community not yet ripe for stripping the States of their powers, even such as might not be requisite for local purposes."[83] Wilson's proposal was rejected by an 8 to 2 vote.

The final plan for the Electoral College followed Ellsworth's proposal and left the mode of selecting the Electors in the hands of the State legislatures. In the case of a tie or if no person received a majority in the Electoral College, the House of Representatives would choose the president *by State*. The Twelfth Amendment altered the original language of Article II, Section 1, Clause 3 by mandating that Electors choose individuals for both president and vice-president, but it retained the requirement that the president be chosen *by State* in case of a tie or the failure of a clear majority winner. Very few members of the founding generation considered the American public as an amorphous "people"; they were the people of the *States*, and the States have a clear role in the Constitution from beginning to end, including the selection of president.

With this in mind, the National Popular Vote Bill *is* constitutional, but it destroys the role of the States, forces Americans into a "one people" mentality, and, from the Founders' point of view, opens the door to pure demagoguery. Both Maine and Nebraska have adopted a system where the Electors are chosen by congressional districts with two "at-large" Electors given to the overall winner of the State. This mode preserves the role of the States in the selection of the president and coincides with the way several States in the late founding period handled the issue. Most States during the time of the founding generation allowed the State legislatures to choose their Electors with a select few adopting the "winner take all" system that most use today. At minimum, any reform should avoid "stripping the States of their powers."

It is a myth—but one often repeated—that the Framers "really wanted" the president to be chosen by the people at large; supposedly they rejected this method *only* because the people in one State would not know enough about candidates from other States. But the records from the Philadelphia Convention clearly illustrate that the Founders intended the Electoral College to be a buffer against the potential abuses of democracy. Several members of the Philadelphia Convention warned against a popularly elected "king" as being dangerous to the liberty of the people. They did not want a demagogue, a despot, or a tyrant, and thought it was better to have an appointed executive than one who would flatter the people for votes.

The popular vote was not tallied until 1824, the first year a member of the founding generation was not among the list of candidates for president. That clearly shows what little regard the founding generation had for the people at large in the election process. George Mason wondered aloud during the Philadelphia Convention if a presidential election should be "performed by those who know least…."[84] Perhaps this question should still be considered.

In Federalist No. 69, Alexander Hamilton carefully detailed the differences between the king of Great Britain and the president of the United States. His purpose was to show how no parallels existed between the two executives and that Americans had nothing to fear from the executive branch. For example, Hamilton wrote that the president served a four-year term while the king was an "*hereditary monarch*"; the president could be impeached and removed from office while the king of Great Britain was "sacred and inviolable"; the president has a qualified veto while the king has "an absolute negative"; the president has a concurrent power with the Senate over appointments and treaties while the king was the "fountain of honor" and the "sole and absolute representative of the nation in all foreign transactions"; the president can command the army and navy, but the king can declare war and raise and regulate fleets and armies "by his own authority"; the president "can prescribe no rules concerning the commerce or currency of the nation: [the king] is in several respects the arbiter of commerce, and in this capacity can establish markets and fairs, can regulate weights and measures, can lay embargoes for a limited time, can coin money, can authorise or prohibit the circulation of foreign coin. The one has no particle of spiritual jurisdiction: The other is the supreme head and Governor of the national church!"[85]

Hamilton was not alone in his sales pitch to the people of the States. Others, such as James Wilson, John Dickinson, Roger Sherman, and James Iredell, argued many of the same points. According to the Constitution *as ratified*, the president has few and defined powers. He is not the chief legislator, does not have unchecked power over the military or foreign policy, cannot rule by decree, and has no control over "the commerce or currency of the nation." Most presidents in the modern era have ignored and violated these constraints. Members of the founding generation feared executive abuse above all else and sought to restrain it as much as possible.

CHAPTER 4

The Judiciary

"The judicial Power of the United States, shall be vested in one supreme Court, and in such inferior Courts as the Congress may from time to time ordain and establish. The Judges, both of the supreme and inferior Courts, shall hold their Offices during good Behaviour, and shall, at stated Times, receive for their Services, a Compensation, which shall not be diminished during their Continuance in Office." **Article III, Section 1.**

Most Americans today see the Supreme Court as an extra-legislative body. The Court is called upon to "decide" what the law is and how it should be interpreted. For example, during her confirmation hearings in 2010, Elena Kagan was pressed by several senators on whether or not she believed in "judicial activism." She skirted the issue, knowing that a solid "yes" might destroy her future seat on the bench, but her answers often implied that she believed that a Supreme Court justice should interpret the law, which is a common misunderstanding. Most of the founding generation thought it was the role of the legislature, which wrote the laws, to also interpret them. The Supreme Court is given specific adjudicating powers in the Constitution; interpreting the law is not one of them.

James Madison's Virginia Plan called for a "National Judiciary" that would consist of "one or more supreme tribunals, and of inferior tribunals to be chosen by the National Legislature...."[1] Madison later remarked that "a Government without a proper Executive and Judiciary would be the mere trunk of a body without arms or legs to act and move."[2] No one objected to a judicial branch and a "Supreme Court." Even William Paterson's New Jersey Plan contained a "supreme Tribunal." The issue, at least initially, was the creation of "inferior courts." These were viewed as a potential affront to State judicial authority.

John Rutledge moved to strike the clause establishing inferior courts. He argued that the "State Tribunals might and ought to be left in all cases to decide in the first instance the right of appeal to the supreme national tribunal being sufficient to secure the national rights & uniformity of Judgments: that it was making an unnecessary encroachment on the jurisdiction of the States, and was creating unnecessary obstacles to their adoption of the new system."[3] Fellow South Carolinian Pierce Butler seconded Rutledge. "The people will not bear such innovations. The States will revolt at such encroachments. Supposing such an establishment to be useful, we must not venture on it. We must follow the example of Solon who gave the Athenians not the best Govt. he could devise; but the best they would receive."[4] Luther Martin said in July 1787 that inferior courts would "create jealousies & oppositions in the State tribunals, with the jurisdiction of which they will interfere."[5] Both Madison and James Wilson altered the language by replacing the *absolute* creation of inferior courts with the *potential* creation of inferior courts. This was accepted by an 8 to 2 vote in June and passed without opposition in July. Still, opponents were building a case against a potentially aggressive and over-reaching federal judiciary.

The most important component of Article III, Clause 1 establishes, at least in theory, the independence of federal judges. They are to hold their "Offices during good Behaviour, and shall, at stated Times, receive for their Services, a Compensation, which shall not be diminished during their Continuance in Office." One of the chief complaints of the colonists in the years before the American War for Independence was that judges were political appointees. An independent judiciary was a cornerstone of nearly every State constitution written in the years immediately after the War.

But if federal judges were independent, they also had to be held accountable. Near the conclusion of the Philadelphia Convention, John Dickinson sought to make federal judges impeachable by the executive on an application by the Senate and House of Representatives. John Rutledge opposed this because he said it would weaken "too much the independence of the judges." Only the delegation from Connecticut supported the motion, but both the Framers and the rest of the founding generation understood that the qualification "during good Behaviour" made federal judges subject to impeachment. Judges who abused their authority or acted in a partisan manner on the bench were not following an independent course; they were following a crooked one and needed to be corrected. As for compensation, the Framers generally agreed that judges should be well paid as a means to keep them independent and less prone to accepting bribes,[6] though inevitably there were dissenters, like Richard Henry Lee, who thought high salaries were more likely to invite corruption than prevent it.[7] And "Brutus" complained that federal judges had too much independence: "There is no power above them, to controul any of their decisions. There is no authority that can remove them, and they cannot be controuled by the laws of the legislature. In short, they are independent of the people, of the legislature, and of every power under heaven. Men placed in this situation will generally soon feel themselves independent of heaven itself."[8]

Alexander Hamilton, in Federalist No. 78, tried to assure doubters by arguing that as long as the judicial power was not married to the executive or the legislative power, it posed no threat to liberty, because, "though individual oppression may now and then proceed from the courts of justice, the general liberty of the people can never be endangered from that quarter: I mean, so long as the judiciary remains truly distinct from both the legislative and executive."[9] This was because the judiciary on its own would be too weak. But as judicial power has grown, the warnings of writers like "Brutus" seem more prescient.

Judicial Power

"The judicial Power shall extend to all Cases, in Law and Equity, arising under this Constitution, the Laws of the United States, and Treaties made, or which shall be made, under their Authority;—to all Cases affecting Ambassadors, other public Ministers and Consuls;—to all Cases of admiralty and maritime Jurisdiction;—to Controversies to which the United States shall be a Party;—to Controversies between two or more States;—between a State and Citizens of another State;—between Citizens of different States;—between Citizens of the same State claiming Lands under Grants of different States, and between a State, or the Citizens thereof, and foreign States, Citizens or Subjects.

"In all Cases affecting Ambassadors, other public Ministers and Consuls, and those in which a State shall be Party, the supreme Court shall have original Jurisdiction. In all the other Cases before mentioned, the supreme Court shall have appellate Jurisdiction, both as to Law and Fact, with such Exceptions, and under such Regulations as the Congress shall make.

"The Trial of all Crimes, except in Cases of Impeachment, shall be by Jury; and such Trial shall be held in the State where the said Crimes shall have been committed; but when not committed within any State, the Trial shall be at such Place or Places as the Congress may by Law have directed." **Article III, Section 2.**

Thomas Jefferson wrote in 1815 that "the question whether the judges are invested with exclusive authority to decide on the constitutionality of a law has been heretofore a subject of consideration with me in the exercise of official duties. Certainly there is not a word in the Constitution which has given that power to them more than to the Executive or Legislative branches."[10] Jefferson was referring to "judicial review," or the process by which the United States Supreme Court determines the constitutionality of federal (and now State) legislation. The first time the Supreme Court ruled a federal law unconstitutional was in 1803 in the *Marbury v. Madison* case. John Marshall wrote in his decision that "it is emphatically the province and duty of the Judicial Department to say what the law is. Those who apply the rule to particular cases must, of necessity, expound and interpret that rule. If two laws conflict with each other, the Courts must decide on the operation of each." Jefferson refuted Marshall's decision, and wrote twenty years later that "this case of 'Marbury *vs.* Madison' is continually cited by bench and bar, as if it were settled law, without any animadversion on its being an *obiter* dissertation of the Chief Justice."[11] While never directly addressed during the Philadelphia Convention, "judicial review" was alluded to on several occasions. In June 1787, Elbridge Gerry said that "in some States the Judges had actually set aside laws as being against the Constitution." Rufus King believed this was entirely proper, arguing that "the Judges ought to be able to expound the law as it should come before them." But Gunning Bedford opposed any check on the legislature. "The Representatives of the People were the best judges of what was for their interest, and ought to be under no external controul whatever."[12]

John Mercer from Virginia remarked that he "disapproved of the doctrine, that the judges, as expositors of the Constitution, should have authority to declare a law void. He thought laws ought to be well and cautiously made, and then to be uncontrollable." John Dickinson said he was "impressed with the remark of Mr. Mercer, as to the power of the judges to set aside the law. He thought no such power ought to exist. He was at the same time, at a loss what expedient to substitute."[13] Even James Madison had doubts about expansive judicial power. He thought the Convention may have been going "too far, to extend the jurisdiction of the court generally to cases arising under the Constitution, and whether it ought not to be limited to cases of a judiciary nature. The right of expounding the Constitution, in cases not of this nature, ought not to be given to that department."[14]

In broad terms, the delegates from Massachusetts supported "judicial review," while those from Virginia and Delaware rejected it, perhaps because the constitution of Massachusetts allowed a similar practice, while the Virginia constitution prohibited it. Proponents of the Constitution generally contended that the Supreme Court was designed to be a check against unconstitutional *federal* legislation. This did not mean that other branches of government, namely the executive branch, did not have a similar function, but the federal judiciary was trumpeted as the final arbiter in most cases. James Wilson, speaking in the Pennsylvania Ratifying Convention, said, "If a law should be made inconsistent with those powers vested by this instrument in Congress, the judges, as a consequence of their independence, and the particular powers of government being defined, will declare such law to be null and void; for the power of the Constitution predominates. Any thing, therefore, that shall be enacted by Congress contrary thereto, will not have the force of law."[15] Oliver Ellsworth said in the Connecticut Ratifying Convention that "if the general legislature should at any time overleap their limits, the judicial department is a constitutional check. If the United States go beyond their powers, if they make a law which the Constitution does not authorize, it is void; and the judicial power, the national judges, who to secure their impartiality, are to be made independent, will declare it to be void."[16] William Richardson Davie argued in the First North Carolina Ratifying Convention that the "judicial power should be coextensive with the legislative" in order to "correct and counteract" bad laws.[17]

The most spirited debate on this issue took place in the Virginia Ratifying Convention. Patrick Henry and George Mason fired both barrels at the federal judiciary, with Henry calling it "impracticable, or, if reducible to practice, dangerous in the extreme." Both Henry and Mason worried that the federal courts would destroy the State judiciaries. Henry called the State judiciary "the sole protection against a tyrannical execution of the laws," worried that the power of the federal judiciary could not be tempered,[18] and feared it would take on the power to void federal legislation and possibly State legislation.

John Marshall, who had spoken little during the Virginia Convention to that point, rose and began a systematic defense of the federal judiciary. In doing so, he foreshadowed, at least in part, the actions he would take as Chief Justice of the Supreme Court several years later, particularly in regard to "judicial review." Marshall asked Henry if the Congress could "make laws on every subject? Can they make laws affecting the mode of transferring property, or contracts, or claims, between citizens of the same state? Can they go beyond the delegated powers? If they were to make a law not warranted by any of the powers enumerated, it would be considered by the judges as an infringement of the Constitution which they are to guard. They would not consider such a law as coming under their jurisdiction. They would declare it void."[19] This was an important point. Marshall outlined "judicial review"—in fact, he later called the federal judiciary the only "protection from an infringement on the Constitution"[20]—but he also reassured Henry, Mason, and fellow opponent of the Constitution William Grayson that the central judiciary would not overstep its power and rule on cases in which it had no jurisdiction, namely State law.

Perceptive opponents of the judiciary noted that review of federal law was not the issue, though they did hope that there would be some check (either executive or judicial) on bad legislation. The real problem was the role of the general judiciary in regard to State law. That, they said, should have remained outside federal jurisdiction. In essence, they did not want the general government to have the power to declare a State law void unless it violated Article I, Section 10. George Mason argued that the vague language of Article III, Section 2 could lead to only one conclusion: "their [the judiciary's] effect and operation will be utterly to destroy the state governments; for they will be the judges how far their laws operate.... To those who think that one national, consolidated government is best for America, this extensive judicial authority will be agreeable; but I hope there are many in this Convention of a different opinion, and who see their political happiness resting on their state governments." Later, he reiterated that the "greater part" of judicial powers "are unnecessary, and dangerous, as tending to impair, and ultimately destroy, the state judiciaries, and, by the same principle, the legislation of the state governments."[21]

"Brutus" argued that the Framers designed the judicial branch to validate all laws by the general legislature. The two would work in concert to destroy liberty and subvert the State governments. In his twelfth essay, he wrote, "I might instance a number of clauses in the constitution, which, if explained in an *equitable* manner, would extend the powers of the government to every case, and reduce the state legislatures to nothing; but, I should draw out my remarks to an undue length, and I presume enough has been said to shew, that the courts have sufficient ground in the exercise of this power, to determine, that the legislature have no bounds set to them by this constitution, by any supposed right the legislatures of the respective states may have, to regulate any of their local concerns." This was painfully obvious to him.

> These courts will have the authority to decide upon the validity of the laws of any of the states, in all cases where they come in question before them. Where the constitution gives the general government exclusive jurisdiction, they will adjudge all laws made by the states…void *ab initio*. Where the constitution gives them concurrent jurisdiction, the laws of the United States must prevail, because they are the supreme law. In such cases, therefore, the laws of the state legislatures must be repealed, restricted, or so construed, as to give full effect to the laws of the union on the same subject. From these remarks it is easy to see, that in proportion as the general government acquires power and jurisdiction, by the liberal construction which the judges may give the constitution, will those of the states lose its rights, until they become so trifling and unimportant, as not to be worth having.[22]

The idea that the general government should have a right to void State legislation had been debated and repeatedly defeated since the early sessions of the Philadelphia Convention. Charles Pinckney was its most vocal champion. In both July and August 1787, he proposed that the legislature of the United States be vested with the power to "negative all laws passed by the several states, interfering, in the opinions of the legislature, with the general interests and harmony of the Union...."[23] Luther Martin called this power "improper & inadmissible."[24] George Mason questioned if this power would "sit constantly, in order to receive and revise the state laws?" John Rutledge declared "If nothing else, this alone would damn, and ought to damn, the Constitution. Will any state ever agree to be bound hand and foot in this manner? It is worse than making mere corporations of them, whose by-laws would not be subject to this shackle." Only James Wilson emphatically supported the proposal.[25]

Pinckney's proposal did not even make it to committee, and a majority of the Framers shot down every attempt by the nationalists in the Philadelphia Convention to place the general government in a position to overrule State law. Even John Marshall argued that the federal judiciary would not destroy the State courts or unnecessarily enlarge federal power. "The state courts will not lose their jurisdiction of the cases they now decide. They have a concurrence of jurisdiction with the federal courts in those cases in which the latter have cognizance."[26] Of course, less than twenty-five years later, Marshall, as Chief Justice, wrote the majority opinion in *Fletcher v. Peck*, a decision that declared a State law unconstitutional under the dubious claim that Georgia had violated Article I, Section 10, which lists what States cannot do; even then the decision was controversial.

During the Virginia Ratifying Convention, George Mason proposed an amendment that would have replaced the arguably vague grant of judicial powers found in Article III, Section 2, Clause 1, with a far more specific and limited list in order to guard the States' independence from the federal judiciary.[27] The amendment was voted down as unnecessary.

The record of the Philadelphia Convention and the State Ratifying Conventions illustrates that the founding generation believed the Supreme Court would have the ability to void *federal* legislation, meaning "judicial review" was not fabricated out of thin air. However, the Court's ability to declare *State* law unconstitutional is a bit murkier, because the majority of the Founders opposed it, except in a very limited sense. According to the Constitution *as ratified*, the federal courts had limited authority to declare State law void. Essentially, if a State did not violate Article I, Section 10, it could do as it pleased. William Richardson Davie emphasized this in the First North Carolina Ratifying Convention. "There is no instance that can be pointed out wherein the internal policy of the state can be affected by the judiciary of the United States."[28] And Archibald Maclaine said in the same Convention, "The state courts have exclusive jurisdiction over every other possible controversy that can arise between the inhabitants of their own states; nor can the federal courts intermeddle with such disputes, either originally or by appeal."[29] It was only through happenstance that one of the greatest proponents of federal judicial power became Chief Justice of the Supreme Court, and even Marshall had reassured members of his own Ratifying Convention that the States had nothing to fear from the federal courts.

Ultimately, through the Eleventh Amendment to the Constitution, ratified in 1798, the States removed the possibility of being sued in federal court without their consent. This was intended to be the final check on federal judicial jurisdiction vis-à-vis the States, but both the federal courts and the Congress have continually attempted to usurp this power.

CHAPTER 5

Miscellaneous Subjects

Property

"Full Faith and Credit shall be given in each State to the public Acts, Records, and judicial Proceedings of every other State. And the Congress may by general Laws prescribe the Manner in which such Acts, Records, and Proceedings shall be proved, and the Effect thereof." **Article IV, Section 1.**

"The Citizens of each State shall be entitled to all Privileges and Immunities of Citizens in the several States." **Article IV, Section 2, Clause 1.**

In 1996, Congress passed the Defense of Marriage Act, a law that both defined marriage as between one man and one woman and allowed States to refuse to recognize same-sex unions from other States. President Barack Obama and United States Attorney General Eric Holder determined in 2011 that they would no longer enforce the law and declared it unconstitutional. Critics of the law have long pointed to the "Full Faith and Credit Clause" found in Article IV, Section 1, and the "Privileges and Immunities Clause" in Article IV, Section 2, Clause 1 (and in the Fourteenth Amendment), as proof that the law violates the Constitution. This would require a very loose interpretation of both clauses. According to the Constitution as ratified, these two clauses amounted to little more than a protection of private property rights. They did not extend to marriage, civil rights or liberties, travel, or any other restriction on personal freedom as per State law.

Both clauses were lifted from the Articles of Confederation, and in both cases, their intent was clear. During the American War for Independence, several States confiscated the property of British loyalists. As per the Treaty of Paris of 1783, that property was to be returned, but most States refused to comply. Moreover, many men who invested heavily in the War effort ended up going broke. Often bankruptcies and property liens were difficult to enforce if the party moved to another State or if the bulk of their property was located in another State. At the same time, citizens of one State could be prevented from purchasing property in another, or could be given higher taxes due to their "foreign" status. These two clauses allowed the States to use the legal decisions of another State in their courts and protected property rights of the citizens of one State residing for a time in another.

William Johnson and James Wilson said during the Philadelphia Convention, that they "supposed the meaning [of Article IV, Section 1] to be that Judgments in one State should be the ground of actions in other States, & that acts of the Legislatures should be included, for the sake of Acts of insolvency &c...." Charles Pinckney then proposed that a bankruptcy provision should be added to the Constitution. Madison wanted to expand the "Full Faith and Credit" power further, but John Rutledge rebuffed his attempt, claiming that "there was no instance of one nation [State] executing judgments of the Courts of another nation [State]."[1] The "Full Faith and Credit Clause" was intended solely to cover issues involving property.

The same can almost be said for the "Privileges and Immunities Clause," which was written both for the protection of property rights and to make sure that fugitives could not flee from the justice of another State. Madison, in fact, thought of proposing an addition to the clause which would have given property owners a constitutional protection for moving property from one State to another. "Every citizen having an estate in two or more States shall have a right to remove his property from one State to another."[2]

The "General Welfare Clause," the "Privileges and Immunities Clause," and the "Full Faith and Credit Clause" carried virtually the same meaning as they did under the Articles of Confederation. Richard Henry Lee, in arguing against the ratification of the Constitution, defended the Articles of Confederation, in part, on these terms. The Articles, he said, already provided for reciprocal "privileges and immunities" between the citizens of each State, and "full faith and credit" was given to the acts of State in the Union.[3] If the clauses are interpreted this way—and this is how the founding generation interpreted them—then they add nothing to American constitutionalism, but are a mere carryover from the Articles of Confederation, and expansive arguments used by later interpretations of Article IV, Sections 1 and 2 do not comport with the Constitution *as ratified*.

The States

"New States may be admitted by the Congress into this Union; but no new State shall be formed or erected within the Jurisdiction of any other State; nor any State be formed by the Junction of two or more States, or Parts of States, without the Consent of the Legislatures of the States concerned as well as of the Congress." **Article IV, Section 3, Clause 1.**

"The United States shall guarantee to every State in this Union a Republican Form of Government, and shall protect each of them against Invasion; and on Application of the Legislature, or of the Executive (when the Legislature cannot be convened) against domestic Violence." **Article IV, Section 4.**

These two often overlooked clauses were essential to the future of the United States. With vast western lands just over the Appalachian Mountains, North America seemed to be a limitless bounty. Several States already claimed much of the territory to the Mississippi, and there were already Americans who believed the United States would stretch across North America. The method of organizing this territory and admitting new States became an ongoing discussion in the early years of the federal republic. Virginia began the process by giving its western lands to the United States in 1784. The general government under the Articles of Confederation began organizing the territory through the Land Ordinance of 1785 and the Northwest Ordinance of 1787.

In 1789, the First Congress under the Constitution reaffirmed the Northwest Ordinance. According to Article 5 of the Ordinance, "And, whenever any of the said States shall have sixty thousand free inhabitants therein, such State shall be admitted, by its delegates, into the Congress of the United States, on an equal footing with the original States in all respects whatever, and shall be at liberty to form a permanent constitution and State government: Provided, the constitution and government so to be formed, shall be republican, and in conformity to the principles contained in these articles...."[4] The debate over Article IV, Section 3, Clause 1, focused on the equality of the new States.

Gouverneur Morris opposed granting equality to new Western States because he thought their growing numbers would spell political doom for the Eastern States. Arguing against Morris were Madison, George Mason, and Roger Sherman. Madison insisted that "the Western States neither would nor ought to submit to a Union which degraded them from an equal rank with the other States." Morris said his greatest fear was throwing "the power into their [the Western States'] hands."[5]

This subject came to a head in 1803 with the Louisiana Purchase. Jefferson believed that the United States did not have the constitutional authority to buy what amounted to a third of the North American continent from France or admit new territory to the United States. He wrote a proposed amendment to the Constitution that would have allowed for the acquisition of the territory and would have placed its white inhabitants "on the same footing with other citizens of the U.S. in analogous situations."[6] Madison insisted that this was unnecessary and Jefferson shelved his amendment.

Morris wrote privately that he thought the acquisition was unconstitutional and told a friend that "I always thought that, when we should acquire Canada and Louisiana it would be proper to govern them as provinces, and allow them no voice in our councils. In wording the third section of the fourth article [establishing the rules for admitting new states], I went as far as circumstances would permit to establish the exclusion. Candor obliges me to add my belief, that, had it [the argument for exclusion] been more pointedly expressed, a strong opposition [to his position] would have been made."[7]

Men like Morris feared a confederacy of Southern and Western States that would be hostile to the East. But as the First Congress's affirmation of the Northwest Ordinance made clear, the majority of the founding generation believed in the equality of new States; and Jefferson, for one, privately dismissed fears of Western hostility, taking a libertarian view, writing, "The future inhabitants of the Atlantic and Mississippi States will be our sons.... We think we see their happiness in their union, and we wish it. Events may prove it otherwise; and if they see their interest in separation, why should we take side with our Atlantic rather than our Mississippi descendants. It is the elder and the younger son differing. God bless them both, and keep them in union, if it be for their good, but separate them, if it be better."[8]

Article IV, Section 4, addressed much the same issue, namely the sovereignty of the States and their status in the Union. Opponents of the language argued that it abridged the sovereignty of the States by allowing the general government to forcibly apply a

"Republican Form of Government" to each State. William Symmes of Massachusetts wrote: "What Congress may see in our present constitutions, or any future amendments, not strictly republican *in their opinions*, who can tell?—Besides, it is of no importance to any State how ye. govt. in any other is administered, whether by a single House, or by two & a King.—I therefore presume that as this clause meddles too much with ye. independence of ye. several States, so also it answers no valuable end to any, or to ye. whole."[9]

When this Article was debated in the Philadelphia Convention, Luther Martin, Elbridge Gerry, and George Mason sought to lessen the general government's coercive power over the States. Their arguments led to the Constitution's provision that the general government cannot invade a State with the standing army to put down "domestic violence" unless the elected members of the State request intervention.

The driving force behind Article IV, Section 4, was the threat of a foreign power instigating rebellion in the States and using it as a means to seize the government or destroy the Union. As Tench Coxe wrote, "The United States guarantee to every state in the union a separate republican form of government. From thence it follows, that any man or body of men, however rich or powerful, who shall make an alteration in the form of government of any state, whereby the powers thereof shall be attempted to be taken out of the hands of the people at large, will stand guilty of high treason; or should a foreign power seduce or over-awe the people of any state, so as to cause them to vest in the families of any ambitious citizens or foreigners the powers of hereditary governors, whether as Kings or Nobles, that such investment of powers would be void in itself, and every person attempting to execute them would also be guilty of treason."[10] Madison said in the Virginia

Ratifying Convention that "without a general controlling power to call forth the strength of the Union to repel invasions, the country might be overrun and conquered by foreign enemies...."[11]

Even Hamilton argued in Federalist No. 21 that the people of the States had nothing to fear from the Article. "The inordinate pride of State importance has suggested to some minds an objection to the principle of a guarantee in the foederal Government; as involving an officious interference in the domestic concerns of the members. A scruple of this kind would deprive us of one of the principal advantages to be expected from Union; and can only flow from a misapprehension of the nature of the provision itself. It could be no impediment to reforms of the State Constitutions by a majority of the people in a legal and peaceable mode. This right would remain undiminished. The guarantee could only operate against changes to be effected by violence."[12] As usual, however, what Hamilton said in 1787 in selling the Constitution to the States is not what Hamilton did once in power.

The best example is the Whiskey Rebellion of 1794. This was a purposeful provocation of Western Pennsylvania distillers orchestrated by Hamilton in order to showcase the superiority of the general government. Several thousand men marched on Pittsburgh in the summer of 1794 in order to demand redress and harass the tax collectors, who they believed were enforcing an illegal and unpopular tax. Alexander Hamilton, as Secretary of the Treasury, and President George Washington determined, before hearing news of the march on Pittsburgh, to raise an army and put down the "rebellion." There was only one problem. The governor of Pennsylvania, Thomas Mifflin, a hero of the American War for Independence and a signer of the Constitution, did not request federal intervention, nor did the legislature of the State. When Washington personally led the army to Western Pennsylvania in the summer of 1794, he violated Article IV, Section 4, and gave one-time opponents of the Constitution an "I told you so" moment. Both Madison and Jefferson chastised Washington's actions. Madison asserted that the whole event was to "establish the principle that a standing army was necessary for *enforcing the laws*."[13] William Findley argued, in a detailed study of the event published two years after the fact, that the rebellion could have been subdued by the State authorities and federal intervention was unnecessary.[14]

Yet, Washington established a precedent that allowed Abraham Lincoln to send the army into the Southern States in 1861 without a request from the legislatures or from the executives of those States. He also violated Article IV of the Constitution *as ratified*. During the Philadelphia Convention, Luther Martin argued that "the consent of the State ought to precede the introduction of any extraneous force whatever."[15] His opinion was shared by the majority of the Convention. Article IV, Section 4 was not a blank check for the general government to wage war upon the States. As the Article was written and ratified, the States still had the final authority in their domestic concerns.

Supremacy

"This Constitution, and the Laws of the United States which shall be made in Pursuance thereof; and all Treaties made, or which shall be made, under the Authority of the United States, shall be the supreme Law of the Land; and the Judges in every State shall be bound thereby, any Thing in the Constitution or Laws of any State to the Contrary notwithstanding." **Article VI, Clause 2.**

The "Supremacy Clause" found in Article VI is one of the most abused, misunderstood, and misquoted clauses in the Constitution. For example, in February 2011, the Attorney General of North Carolina, Roy Cooper, issued a statement attacking North Carolina House Bill No. 2—a bill that would, if signed into law, ultimately exempt the people of North Carolina from the 2010 federal health-care legislation known as the Patient Protection and Affordable Care Act—on the basis that it violated the "Supremacy Clause" of the Constitution. His Solicitor General, Christopher Browning Jr., wrote, "House Bill 2 violates the Supremacy Clause of the United States Constitution. U.S. Const. art VI, cl. 2 (the 'Constitution and the laws of the United States...shall be the supreme law of the land...anything in the constitution or laws of any state to the contrary notwithstanding')."[16] At first glance, it might appear Browning and Cooper have a case, but in fact they both are guilty of selective quoting. The ellipsis between "United States" and "shall" conveniently omits the most important part of the clause, namely only laws which are made "in Pursuance" of the Constitution are supreme. According to the powers listed in Article I, Section 8, insurance mandates (not to mention all the other parts of the health care bill) are not to be included in the enumerated powers of Congress. The Patient Protection and Affordable Care Act is actually itself unconstitutional, legally unenforceable (if we stick to the meaning of the Constitution as ratified), and cannot be considered "supreme."

The "Supremacy Clause" found its way into the Constitution during debate over the ability of the general government to void State law. That was unacceptable, but the Framers did not want the States to be able to completely run roughshod over the general government. In July 1787, Luther Martin moved that the Convention approve the following resolution: "That the Legislative acts of the U.S. made by virtue & in pursuance of the articles of Union, and all treaties made & ratified under the authority of the U.S. shall be the supreme law of the respective States, as far as those acts or treaties shall relate to the said States, or the Citizens and inhabitants—& that the Judiciaries of the several States shall be bound thereby in their decisions, any thing in the respective laws of the individual States to the contrary notwithstanding." It passed unanimously. John Rutledge altered the language in August, but it carried the same meaning and was likewise unanimously passed.[17] It was never intended to act as a negative on State law.

Opponents of the Constitution nevertheless worried—presciently as it turned out—that this was where the "Supremacy Clause" would lead. Richard Henry Lee wrote in October 1787 that "wherever this constitution, or any part of it, shall be incompatible with the ancient customs, rights, the laws or the constitutions heretofore established in the United States, it will entirely abolish them and do them away: And not only this, but the laws of the United States which shall be made in pursuance of the federal constitution will be also supreme laws, and wherever they shall be incompatible with those customs, rights, laws or constitutions heretofore established, they will also entirely abolish them and do them away."[18] Arthur Lee, Richard Henry Lee's brother, wrote in November 1787 that "this new system, with one sweeping clause, bears down on every constitution in the union, and establishes its arbitrary doctrines, supreme and paramount to all the bills and declarations of rights, in which we vainly put our trust, and on which we rested the security of our often declared, unalienable liberties. But I trust the whole people of this country, will unite, in crying out, as did our sturdy ancestors of old—*Nolumus leges anglicae mutari* [we do not want the laws of England changed]—We will not part with our birthright."[19]

George Bryan of Pennsylvania, writing as "The Centinel," found no solace in the phrase "pursuant to the constitution." This was, he said, "no restriction to the authority of congress; for the foregoing sections give them unlimited legislation."[20] A minority of the Philadelphia Ratifying Convention agreed with him, stating:

> It has been alleged that the words "pursuant to the constitution," are a restriction upon the authority of Congress; but when it is considered that by other sections they are invested with every efficient power of government, and which may be exercised to the absolute destruction of the state governments, without any violation of even the forms of the constitution, this seeming restriction, as well as every other restriction in it, appears to us to be nugatory and delusive; and only introduced as a blind upon the real nature of the government. In our opinion, "pursuant to the constitution," will be co-extensive with the *will* and *pleasure* of Congress, which, indeed, will be the only limitation on their powers.[21]

Luther Martin, in his address to the "Citizens of Maryland" in March 1788, said that he wrote the original version of the "Supremacy Clause" specifically to guard against the general government capriciously voiding State law. He did not, however, support the "Supremacy Clause" as written in Article VI. In his mind, his language would have preserved the sovereignty of the States, particularly in regard to State constitutions and bills of rights. Martin argued that the final version "would amount to a total and unconditional surrender to that [general] government, by the citizens of this state, of every right and privilege secured to them by our constitution, and an express compact and stipulation with the general government, that it may, at its discretion, make laws in direct violation of those rights."[22]

The "Supremacy Clause" took center stage in many of the State ratification debates. George Mason told the Virginia Ratifying Convention that "if the laws and constitution of the general government, as expressly said, be paramount to those of any state, are not those rights with which we were afraid to trust our own citizens annuled and given up to the general government? ... If they are not given up, where are they secured? By implication? Let gentlemen shew that they are secured in a plain, direct, unequivocal manner.... If a check be necessary in our own state government, it is much more so in a government where our representatives are to be at the distance of 1000 miles from us without any responsibility."[23] Timothy Bloodworth of North Carolina declared in his State Ratifying Convention that Article VI "appears to me to sweep off all the constitutions of the states. It is a total repeal of every act and constitution of the states. The judges are sworn to uphold it. It will produce an abolition of the state governments. Its sovereignty absolutely annihilates them."[24]

Beating back the attacks on the "Supremacy Clause" would be one of the keys to ratification. That responsibility was given, in part, to Alexander Hamilton. During the New York Ratifying Convention, Alexander Hamilton promised that the "supreme legislature has only general powers, and the civil and domestic concerns of the people are regulated by the laws of the several states.... [The State governments] are absolutely necessary to the system. Their existence must form a leading principle in the most perfect constitution we could form." He called attacks on the Supremacy

Clause "curious sophistry" and argued that the "laws of the United States are supreme, as to all their proper, constitutional objects: the laws of the states are supreme in the same way. These supreme laws may act on different objects without clashing, or they may operate on different parts of the same object, with perfect harmony." Hamilton concluded that the Constitution was "framed upon truly republican principles; and that, as it is expressly designed to provide for the common protection and the general welfare of the United States, it must be utterly repugnant to this Constitution to subvert the state governments, or oppress the people."[25]

When pressed the following day, Hamilton summarized the Supremacy Clause in three sentences: "I maintain that the word *supreme* imports no more than this—that the Constitution, and laws made in pursuance thereof, cannot be controlled or defeated by any other law. The acts of the United States, therefore, will be absolutely obligatory as to all the proper objects and powers of the general government...*but the laws of Congress are restricted to a certain sphere, and when they depart from this sphere, they are no longer supreme or binding*"[26] (emphasis added). This is how proponents of the Constitution insisted that "in pursuance thereof" would be interpreted: the States and the people would not be obligated to follow unconstitutional acts, and any law that exceeded the enumerated powers of the Constitution was void. Hamilton emphasized this point in Federalist No. 33, when he wrote, "It will not, I presume, have escaped observation that it *expressly* confines this supremacy to laws made *pursuant to the Constitution*...."[27]

Hamilton's arguments coincided with one of the more important essays in the Federalist. James Madison wrote in Federalist No. 45 that "the powers delegated by the proposed Constitution to the federal government are few and defined. Those which are to remain in the State governments are numerous and indefinite. The former will be exercised principally on external objects, as war, peace, negotiation, and foreign commerce; with which last the power of taxation will, for the most part, be connected. The powers reserved to the several States will extend to all the objects which, in the ordinary course of affairs, concern the lives, liberties, and properties of the people, and the internal order, improvement, and prosperity of the State."[28] This is often called "dual federalism" and was the principal defense against attacks on the "Supremacy Clause." The States were supreme in regard to their reserved powers, the central government in the general concerns of the Union of the States. In Federalist No. 46 Madison said that "the powers proposed to be lodged in the federal government are as little formidable to those reserved to the individual States, as they are indispensably necessary to accomplish the purposes of the Union."[29]

Though today they are considered the most conspicuous proponents of the Constitution, Madison and Hamilton were not alone in their interpretation of the "Supremacy Clause." Noah Webster, writing as "America" in response to the minority in the Pennsylvania Convention, said in 1787 that "you know that the powers of the Congress are defined, to extend only to those matters which are in their nature and effects, *general*. You know, the Congress cannot meddle with the internal police of any State, or abridge its Sovereignty. And you know, at the same time, that in all general concerns, the laws of Congress must be *supreme* or they must be *nothing*."[30] Thomas McKean, one of the foremost proponents of the Constitution in Pennsylvania, said in the State Ratifying Convention, "The meaning [of the Supremacy Clause] which appears to be plain and well expressed is simply this, that Congress have the power of making laws upon any subject over which the proposed plan gives them a jurisdiction, and that those laws, thus made in pursuance of the Constitution, shall be binding upon the states."[31] In other words, the general government could not encroach on the rights of the States, because Congress had to abide by its "jurisdiction" (its enumerated powers) in making laws in "pursuance of the Constitution."

James Iredell said essentially the same thing in the First North Carolina Ratifying Convention. "When Congress passes a law consistent with the Constitution, it is to be binding on the people. If Congress, under pretense of executing one power, should, in fact, usurp another, they will violate the Constitution."[32] Roger Sherman wrote in December 1787, "One excellency of the constitution is that when the government of the united States acts within its proper bounds it will be the interest of the legislatures of the particular States to Support it, but when it over leaps those bounds and interferes with the rights of the State governments they will be powerful enough to check it...."[33] Pelatiah Webster, a Pennsylvania Federalist, had the most interesting defense of the "Supremacy Clause." Writing as "A Citizen of Philadelphia" in November 1787, Webster contended that critics like "Brutus" had no reason to fear the Constitution because:

> The new Constitution leaves all the Thirteen States, complete republics, as it found them, but all confederated under the direction and controul of a federal head, for certain defined national purposes only, *i.e.* it leaves all the dignities, authorities, and internal police of each State in free, full, and perfect condition; unless when national purposes make the countroul of them by the federal head, or authority, necessary to the general

benefit. These powers of controul by the federal head or authority, are *defined* in the new constitution, as minutely as may be, in their principle....[34]

It is clear, then, that the "Supremacy Clause" made the general government supreme only in regard to its "*defined*" powers, the States retained their sovereignty in regard to all powers not granted to the general government, and if the general government violated the Constitution, the States were meant to apply a check on the general government.

How the States would "check it" became the principle problem. Oliver Ellsworth, John Marshall, and other proponents of "judicial review" put their faith in the Supreme Court. But what if Congress passed an unconstitutional law, the executive signed it, and the Court became complicit in the usurpation of State authority by refusing to void it? The arguments that were used in *defense* of the "Supremacy Clause" helped establish the foundation of what later became known as nullification or State interposition. If, as Hamilton, Madison, Iredell, Webster, Sherman, McKean, and others said, unconstitutional laws were "no longer supreme or binding," and if "the Congress cannot meddle with the internal police of any State, or abridge its Sovereignty," then it would follow that the people of the States acting through their sovereign State legislatures could void such a law. That is exactly what Madison and Thomas Jefferson said in the Virginia and Kentucky Resolutions of 1798.

Jefferson, the author of the Kentucky Resolves, wrote:

That the several States composing, the United States of America, are not united on the principle of unlimited submission to their general government; but that, by a

compact under the style and title of a Constitution for
the United States, and of amendments thereto, they
constituted a general government for special purposes—delegated to that government certain definite
powers, reserving, each State to itself, the residuary
mass of right to their own self-government; and that
whensoever the general government assumes undele-
gated powers, its acts are unauthoritative, void, and of
no force: that to this compact each State acceded as a
State, and is an integral part, its co-States forming, as
to itself, the other party: that the government created
by this compact was not made the exclusive or final
judge of the extent of the powers delegated to itself;
since that would have made its discretion, and not the
Constitution, the measure of its powers; but that, as in
all other cases of compact among powers having no
common judge, *each party has an equal right to judge
for itself, as well of infractions as of the mode and measure
of redress.*[35]

Madison, though softer in tone, followed suit in the Virginia
Resolves:

That this Assembly doth explicitly and peremptorily
declare, that it views the powers of the federal government, as resulting from the compact, to which the states
are parties; as limited by the plain sense and intention
of the instrument constituting the compact; as no further valid that they are authorized by the grants enumerated in that compact; and that in case of a

deliberate, palpable, and dangerous exercise of other powers, not granted by the said compact, the states who are parties thereto, have the right, and are in duty bound, to interpose for arresting the progress of the evil, and for maintaining within their respective limits, the authorities, rights and liberties appertaining to them.[36]

Their primary target was the blatantly unconstitutional Sedition Act of 1798, but what is important for our discussion is that their arguments mirrored those made by virtually every *defender* of the "Supremacy Clause." Later, "nullification" would be dusted off by States both North and South to void federal usurpations of their power through what they viewed as unconstitutional legislation.[37] Opponents of the Constitution were right that the "Supremacy Clause" would ultimately be used to strike down State sovereignty, but according to the Constitution *as ratified* and as sold to the States, it only applied to *constitutional* federal laws and was never intended to trump the powers reserved to the States.

The Union

"The Ratification of the Conventions of nine States shall be sufficient for the Establishment of this Constitution *between the States so ratifying the Same*" (emphasis added). **Article VII.**

The Constitution is a compact between the States. The States, in convention, ratified it, and it was established "between the States" as Article VII illustrates; the delegates to the Philadelphia

Convention voted by State, not by individual; the States originally elected members of the United States Senate; the States elect members of the Electoral College who in turn elect the president; if a presidential election ends without a clear winner in the Electoral College, members of the House of Representatives vote by State to elect a president; and a State cannot be deprived of its "equal suffrage in the Senate without its consent." The Constitution is littered with features that definitively prove that the document maintains the Union of States—and the Founders' definition of Union is important.

With few exceptions, the founding generation recognized that the States had differing economic, cultural, political, and social norms and interests, not to mention differences on the contentious issue of slavery. On the last day of the Philadelphia Convention, for example, George Mason offered a proviso which would have required a two-thirds majority to pass "a navigation act" before 1808. He argued that leaving the matter to a simple majority, as the Constitution had done, would "enable a few rich merchants in Philadelphia, New York, and Boston, to monopolize the staples [staple exports] of the Southern States, and reduce their value perhaps fifty per cent...." His motion was defeated 7 to 3 on almost purely sectional lines.[38] Earlier in the Convention, Oliver Ellsworth said, "The manners of different states were very different in the style of living, and in the profits accruing from the exercise of like talents."[39] Concerning compliance to militia laws, Ellsworth thought, "Three or four shilling's as a penalty will enforce obedience better in New England, than forty lashes in some other places."[40]

Joseph Taylor of North Carolina questioned whether the people of New England could be trusted. "We see plainly that men who come from New England are different from us. They are ignorant of our situation; they do not know the state of our country. They cannot with safety legislate for us."[41]

In July 1787 Gouverneur Morris spoke of regional differences in terms of what they meant for the Union:

> A distinction has been set up, and urged, between the Northern and Southern States. He had hitherto considered this doctrine as heretical. He still thought the distinction groundless. He sees, however, that it is persisted in; and the southern gentlemen will not be satisfied unless they see the way open to their gaining a majority in the public councils. The consequence of such a transfer of power from the maritime to the interior and landed interest, will, he forsees, be such an oppression to commerce, that he shall be obliged to vote for the vicious principle of equality in the second branch, in order to provide some defense for the Northern States against it. But to come more to the point—either this distinction is fictitious or real; if fictitious, let it be dismissed, and let us proceed with due confidence. If it be real, instead of attempting to blend incompatible things, let us at once take a friendly leave of each other. There can be no end of demands for security, if every particular interest is to be entitled to it.[42]

As the Philadelphia Convention ground to a virtual halt in July 1787, Morris again rose and said he "came here to form a *compact* for the good of America. He was ready to do so with all the states. He hoped and believed that all would enter into such a compact. If they would not, he was ready *to join with any states that would*. But as the *compact* was to be *voluntary*, it is in vain for the Eastern States to insist on what the Southern States will never agree to..."[43] (emphasis added). So, if some States would *not* join in a Union, they would be independent, and Morris recognized that in order to forge a "compact," the States had to compromise or leave issues not of general concern off the table. Morris equated compact to Union, and most of the founding generation viewed the general government in that manner.

Madison labeled the "Federal Union as analogous, not to social compacts among individual men, but to the conventions among individual states." This meant that should one party "breach...any one article...all the other parties are at liberty to consider the whole convention as dissolved, unless they choose rather to compel the delinquent party to repair the breach." Compacts among individuals, Madison insisted, could also be dissolved by a breach of the compact, unless "the contrary is *implied* in the compact itself, and particularly by the law of it which gives an indefinite authority to the majority to bind the whole, in all cases." Madison suggested that the only conclusion to be drawn from this dichotomy was that "we are not to consider the Federal Union as analogous to the social compact of individuals: for if it were so, a majority would have a right to bind the rest, and even to form a new constitution for the whole...."[44]

When Article VII was discussed, Rufus King insisted on inserting the phrase "between the States" to "confine the operation of the Govt. to the States ratifying it."[45] Those that didn't, such as Rhode Island, would not be part of the new government. Even James Wilson said, "As the Constitution stands, the States only which ratify can be bound."[46] Additionally, on the final day of the

Convention, Gouverneur Morris added the second clause of the Article, which began, "Done in Convention by the Unanimous Consent of the States present...." This was done, he said, to "gain the dissenting members," but the language clearly showed that the government was a compact among States. Morris concluded that "the signing, in the form proposed, related only to the fact that *the states* present were unanimous."[47]

As Madison said early in the Convention, the whole could not compel a separate part to comply through force. The delegates to the Philadelphia Convention were writing a new Constitution, but it required the consent of the "conventions" of the States to adopt it. Proponents of the Constitution argued their actions were legal because the Union was a compact and the States could choose to be part of it or not. The Constitution did not alter the form of the Union. It was still a compact "for the United States of America," as under the Articles, but with alterations that strengthened it and made it a "more perfect Union."

The Union was designed to absorb differences among the States, but it could only do that if the central government handled the "general" concerns of the States. Compromise was essential and no one section was supposed to dominate the government. When that did happen—and it did almost immediately after the Constitution was ratified—secession was openly discussed. It was the impending threat of "disunion" in 1787 that forced many reluctant delegates at both the Philadelphia and State Ratifying Conventions to support the Constitution and swallow the pill of compromise in the first place. Edmund Randolph wrote in 1787, "Our very quiet depends upon the duration of the union. Among the upright and intelligent, few can read without emotion the future fate of the states, if severed from each other."[48] Madison, in Federalist No. 41, said that if disunion occurred, "It will present liberty every where crushed between standing armies and perpetual taxes. The fortunes of disunited America will be even more disastrous than those of Europe." Thus, "Every man who loves peace, every man who loves his country, every man who loves liberty, ought to have it ever before his eyes, that he may cherish in his heart a due attachment to the Union of America, and be able to set a due value on the means of preserving it."[49] This was the common argument. If disunion should occur, the result would be constant wars, tyrannical despots, and high taxes. Not everyone in the founding generation, however, recoiled at the prospect of "separate confederacies" or believed that the only way to avoid war, taxes, and tyranny was to adopt the Constitution. Most opponents, in fact, thought the Constitution and centralization would produce these evils, not prevent them.

Before the Philadelphia Convention met in 1787, an opinion piece published in the *New York Daily Advertiser* under the pen-name "Reason" asked, "Instead of attempting one general government for the whole community of the United States, would it not be preferable to distribute the States into three Republics, who should enter into a perpetual League or Alliance for mutual defense." Just days later, "Lycurgus" responded in the same paper that "all political writers of eminence agree, that a republic should not comprehend a large territory...." "Lycurgus" advocated dividing the continent into four republics based on climate and geography. "The religion, manners, customs, exports, imports, and general interest of each, being then the same, no opposition arising from differences in these would any longer divide their councils, unanimity would render us secure at home, and respected abroad, and promote agriculture, manufactures [*sic*], and commerce."[50] Luther Martin remarked during the Philadelphia Convention that "he had rather see partial Confederacies take place, than the plan on the table...."[51]

"Brutus" argued that the United States should never be "one government. The United States includes a variety of climates. The productions of the different parts of the union are very variant, and their interests, of consequence, diverse. Their manners and habits differ as much as their climates and productions; and their sentiments are by no means coincident. The laws and customs of the several states are, in many respects, very diverse, and in some opposite; each would be in favor of its own interests and customs, and, of consequence, a legislature, formed of representatives from the respective parts, would not only be too numerous to act with any care or decision, but would be composed of such heterogenous [*sic*] and discordant principles, as would continually be contending with each other." The only way to avoid this, "Brutus" thought, was to avoid adopting the Constitution and maintain the "thirteen confederated republics" of the United States.[52]

Patrick Henry had the final word on the idea of separate confederacies during the Virginia Ratifying Convention:

> I am persuaded of what the honorable gentleman says, that separate confederacies will ruin us. In my judgment, they are evils never to be thought of till a people are driven by necessity. When he asks my opinion of consolidation, of one power to reign over America with a strong hand, I will tell him I am persuaded of the rectitude of my honorable friend's opinion, (Mr. Mason) that one government cannot reign over so extensive a country as this is, without absolute despotism. Compared to such a consolidation, small

confederacies are little evils; though they ought to be
recurred to but in case of necessity. Virginia and North
Carolina are despised. They could exist separated from
the rest of America. Maryland and Vermont were not
overrun when out of the confederacy....[53]

Rather than keep States within a Union they no longer supported, the Jeffersonians of the early federal period were willing to
accept separate confederacies. When confronted with the prospect
of a New England secession in 1801, Thomas Jefferson said in his
first inaugural address, "If there be any among us who would wish
to dissolve this Union or to change its republican form, let them
stand undisturbed as monuments of the safety with which error
of opinion may be tolerated where reason is left free to combat it."[54]
Jefferson, of course, believed the Union was a blessing, but only in
so far as it preserved the fundamental structure of a federal republic—a Union of States for general purposes, and not a consolidated
government that left the States powerless. For that reason he suggested in 1787 that nine States should ratify the Constitution, but
the others should hold out for amendments that further limited
the power of the general government.

Article VII established a government for the United States
"between the States so ratifying the Same." The Constitution was
and is a compact between the States, or the people of the States in
convention, and the general government was designed to ignore the
obvious differences that existed between States and sections. It was
a "general" government for "general" purposes. Throughout the
months leading to ratification, proponents of the Constitution
constantly argued that the United States would not be consolidated,
the States were ceding only a portion of their sovereignty to the

general government; the States still had a dominant role, particularly in regard to domestic concerns. The "common defense and general welfare" were portrayed as limited objects; the "Necessary and Proper Clause" the "General Welfare Clause," and the "Supremacy Clause" were to be *strictly* interpreted. Had the States not had these assurances, they would not have ratified the Constitution.

CHAPTER 6

Amendments and a Bill of Rights

"The Congress, whenever two thirds of both Houses shall deem it necessary, shall propose Amendments to this Constitution, or, on the Application of the Legislatures of two thirds of the several States, shall call a Convention for proposing Amendments, which, in either Case, shall be valid to all Intents and Purposes, as Part of this Constitution, when ratified by the Legislatures of three fourths of the several States, or by Conventions in three fourths thereof, as the one or the other Mode of Ratification may be proposed by the Congress; Provided that no Amendment which may be made prior to the Year One thousand eight hundred and eight shall in any Manner affect the first and fourth Clauses in the Ninth Section of the first Article; and that no State, without its Consent, shall be deprived of its equal Suffrage in the Senate." **Article V.**

The Constitution would also not have been ratified without the promise of a bill of rights. While it was not explicitly stated as a condition of ratification, three of the most powerful States—New York, Massachusetts, and Virginia—all had sizeable enough minorities with enough political muscle to block ratification had proponents balked at including a bill of rights. Every one of the first ten amendments to the Constitution was born from arguments leveled against the un-amended final draft of the document. In fact, the original Bill of Rights was prefaced with a revealing preamble: "THE Conventions of a number of the States having at the time of their adopting the Constitution, expressed a desire, in order to prevent misconstruction or abuse of its powers, that further declaratory and restrictive clauses should be added: And as extending the ground of public confidence in the Government, will best insure the beneficent ends of its institution."[1] The Bill of Rights is there to check "misconstruction or abuse" of the powers granted to the general government, to make clear the extent of some of the Constitution's arguably vague clauses.

Only four members of the Philadelphia Convention actively pressed for a bill of rights: George Mason, Elbridge Gerry, Luther Martin, and Charles Pinckney (and Pinckney's activity was limited). On 12 September 1787, just five days before the final draft of the Constitution was signed, Mason rose and said a bill of rights, particularly an expressed protection of trial by jury, would "give great quiet to the people." In response, Gerry motioned that a committee be formed to "prepare a Bill of Rights." Roger Sherman immediately rejected it, not because he opposed civil liberties, but because—from a States' Rights perspective—he thought it was unnecessary. "The State Declarations of Rights are not repealed by this Constitution; and being in force are sufficient...." According to Sherman—and most proponents of the Constitution in 1787 and 1788—the general government had delegated powers that could not be enlarged at the expense of the States or the people of the States, and since the Constitution did not expressly give the general government the power to abridge the press or speech or eliminate trial by jury for example, the States retained the ability to protect the civil liberties of the people. Mason disagreed and said, "The Laws of the U.S. are to be paramount to State Bills of Rights." Gerry's motion was defeated 10 to 0, and both he and Mason listed a lack of a bill of rights as one of the primary reasons they refused to sign the Constitution.[2]

Mason's call for a bill of rights became a rallying cry for opponents of the document, and the absence of such a bill was used as evidence that the general government intended to seize the powers of the States and strip civil liberties from the people. Martin said in March 1788 that "had the government been formed upon principles truly federal...legislating over and acting upon the states only in their collective or political capacity, and not on individuals, there would have been no need of a bill of rights, as far as related to the rights of individuals, but only as to the rights of states:—But the proposed constitution being intended and empowered to act not only on states, but also immediately on individuals, it renders a recognition and a stipulation in favour of the rights of both states and of men, not only proper, but...*absolutely* necessary."[3] Benjamin Workman, an Irish immigrant and mathematics tutor at the

University of Pennsylvania, wrote in 1787, "If we adopt this plan of government in its present form; I say that we shall have reason to curse the day that America became independent. Horrid thought! that the greatest blessing God ever bestowed on a nation, should terminate in its misery and disgrace. Strange reverse this! that the freemen of America, *the favored of heaven*, should submit to a government so arbitrary in its embrio [*sic*], that even *a bill of rights* cannot be obtained, to secure to the people their unalienable privileges."[4]

Thomas Tredwell of New York made perhaps the most passionate argument against the Constitution devoid of a bill of rights in the New York Ratifying Convention. He invoked the cause of 1776, and said:

> In this Constitution, sir, we have departed widely from the principles and political faith of '76 when the spirit of liberty ran high, and danger put a curb on ambition. Here we find no security for the rights of individuals, no security for the existence of our state governments; here is no bill of rights, no proper restriction of power; our lives, our property, and our consciences, are left wholly at the mercy of the legislature, and the powers of the judiciary may be extended to any degree short of almighty. Sir, in this Constitution we have not only neglected—we have done worse,—we have openly violated, our faith,—that is, our public faith.[5]

Nathaniel Barrell insisted on amendments because "Congress will be vested with more extensive powers than ever Great Britain exercised over us; too great...to intrust with any class of men...even though composed of such exalted, amiable characters as the great Washington; for, while we consider them as men of like passions, the same spontaneous, inherent thirst for power with ourselves, great and good as they may be, when they enter upon this all-important charge, what security can we have that they will continue so? And, were we sure they would continue the faithful guardians of our liberties, and prevent any infringement on the privileges of the people, what assurance can we have that such men will always hold the reins of government—that their successors will be such?"[6]

Proponents of the Constitution used Sherman's reasoning and turned the argument on its head: a bill of rights, they said, would essentially kill State sovereignty. Hugh Williamson of North Carolina contended that "the citizens of the United States have no more occasion for a second Declaration of Rights, than they have for a section in favor of the press. Their rights, in the several States, have long since been explained and secured by particular declarations, which make a part of their several Constitutions. It is granted, and *perfectly understood*, that under the Government of the Assemblies of the States, and under the Government of the Congress, every right is reserved to the individual, which he has not expressly delegated to this, or that Legislature"[7] (emphasis added). Theophilus Parsons of Massachusetts, one of the primary proponents of the Constitution in that State, echoed Williamson. "Is there a single natural right we enjoy, uncontrolled by our own legislature, that Congress can infringe? Not one. Is there a single political right secured to us by our constitution, against the attempts of our legislature, which we are deprived of by this Constitution? Not one...."[8]

Both James Wilson and Alexander Hamilton called a bill of rights dangerous to the liberty of the people. Wilson said at the

Pennsylvania Ratifying Convention that "a bill of rights would not only be unnecessary, but...highly imprudent. In all societies, there are many powers and rights which cannot be particularly enumerated. A bill of rights annexed to a constitution is *an enumeration of the powers* reserved. If we attempt an enumeration, every thing that is not enumerated is presumed to be given. The consequence is, that an imperfect enumeration would throw all implied power into the scale of the government, and the rights of the people would be rendered incomplete."[9]

Hamilton, in Federalist No. 84, wrote that "a minute detail of particular rights is certainly far less applicable to a constitution like that under consideration, which is merely intended to regulate the general political interests of the nation, than to a constitution which has the regulation of every species of personal and private concerns." Moreover, a bill of rights was "dangerous." "They would contain various exceptions to powers which are not granted; and on this very account, would afford a colourable pretext to claim more than were granted. For why declare that things shall not be done which there is no power to do? Why for instance, should it be said, that the liberty of the press shall not be restrained, when no power is given by which restrictions may be imposed? I will not contend that such a provision would confer a regulating power; but it is evident that it would furnish, to men disposed to usurp, a plausible pretence for claiming that power."[10]

For Hamilton and Wilson, a bill of rights would unreasonably *enlarge* the powers of government, for they both assumed that designing men would arrogate to themselves or to the general government any powers omitted from the enumerated list. This was an interesting argument, because this is precisely what Hamilton would do as Secretary of the Treasury less than three years later, except he expanded on the *delegated* powers in Article I, Section 8, when he proposed for Congress's approval the first national bank. Perhaps he was anticipating his own actions. Regardless, the opponents of the Constitution won the argument, and virtually every State submitted proposals for a bill of rights. Madison ultimately condensed the near two hundred submissions to twelve, and they were ratified by the States in 1791. His arrangement, however, is curious, because they are not in their proposed order. The following is a brief synopsis of the amendments, grouped by relevance, in the general order in which they were proposed by the States.

"The powers not delegated to the United States by the Constitution, nor prohibited by it to the States, are reserved to the States respectively, or to the people." **Amendment X.**

"The enumeration in the Constitution, of certain rights, shall not be construed to deny or disparage others retained by the people." **Amendment IX.**

These two amendments form the backbone of the Bill of Rights. Obviously, they anchor the list, but Amendment Ten was usually the first in the proposed lists from the States. It was designed to check what Patrick Henry called the "sweeping clauses" of the Constitution, namely the "General Welfare Clause," the "Necessary and Proper Clause," and the "Supremacy Clause." Jefferson cited Amendment Ten in his Kentucky Resolves of 1798, and when this amendment was added to the Constitution, those who had opposed the document were generally satisfied that it would act as a hedge against the power of the general government.

Every proposed version either contained the words "expressly" (to limit federal power to the duties expressly given it by the Constitution), "sovereignty" (in the sense of protecting the sovereignty of the States), or "jurisdiction" (in terms of limited federal jurisdiction).

Robert Lansing in New York proposed, "That no power shall be exercised by Congress, but such as is expressly given by this Constitution; and all others, not expressly given, shall be reserved to the respective states, to be by them exercised."[11] North Carolina simply proposed that each State was to "retain every power, jurisdiction, and right, which is not by this Constitution delegated to the Congress of the United States." This was a mere copy of the same amendment that Virginia produced in their Ratifying Convention.[12] Robert Whitehill of Pennsylvania proposed an amendment stating that "the sovereignty, freedom, and independency of the several states shall be retained, and every power, jurisdiction, and right which is not by this constitution expressly delegated to the United States in Congress assembled."[13]

This was the amendment that, as Luther Martin had said, would preserve the "rights of the states." His home State of Maryland proposed, "That Congress shall exercise no power but what is expressly delegated by this Constitution." The Maryland amendment is interesting because it included language that directly expressed its intent: "By this amendment, the general powers given to Congress by the first and last paragraphs of the 8th sct. of art. 1, and the 2nd paragraph of the 6th article, would be in a great measure restrained; those dangerous expressions, by which the bills of rights, and constitutions, of the several states may be repealed by the laws of Congress, in some degree moderated; and the exercise of constructive powers wholly prevented."[14]

The final version more closely resembled that of North Carolina and Virginia, and after the failure of a last ditch effort to insert
the word "expressly" before the word "delegated" (because it was
deemed unnecessary), the Tenth Amendment passed without
debate. The Tenth Amendment's intent was clear. It was viewed as
essential to preserve the sovereignty of the States and to avoid a
consolidated *national* government.

The Ninth Amendment was a direct result of the arguments
leveled against a bill of rights by Hamilton, Sherman, and Wilson.
This was the "catch all" amendment that Martin said was essential
to recognize the rights of men. In contrast to the Tenth Amendment, which protected the States in their collective capacity, the
Ninth Amendment protected individuals and was intended to
address Hamilton's fear that enumerating rights in a bill of rights
would leave an opening for unscrupulous politicians to seize rights
that were not enumerated. Madison said in 1789 during the congressional debates over a bill of rights that Hamilton's argument
was "one of the most plausible...I have ever heard urged against
the admission of a bill of rights into this system; but, I conceive,
that it may be guarded against..." The Ninth Amendment did just
that with its direct statement: "The enumeration in the Constitution, of certain rights, shall not be construed to deny or disparage
others retained by the people."[15] State declarations of rights, which
could be more extensive than the federal Bill of Rights, were thus
protected and served as a barrier against federal power. The Ninth
Amendment was another shield to guard the people from abusive
government.

"Congress shall make no law respecting an establishment of religion, or prohibiting the free exercise

> thereof; or abridging the freedom of speech, or of the press; or the right of the people peaceably to assemble, and to petition the Government for a redress of grievances." **Amendment I.**

The First Amendment is arguably the most famous and most debated amendment in the Bill of Rights. Madison combined five civil liberties into the First in order to condense the various proposals from the State Ratifying Conventions. There are several important components to the First Amendment, not the least of which is the first five words, "Congress shall make no law...." This established a precedent for the next nine amendments and amplified the preamble to the Bill of Rights. They were designed to limit the powers of the general government *only*. States were exempt and could, if the several legislatures wished, pass laws establishing a church, limiting the press, outlawing seditious speech, or restricting the right of assemblage. Madison attempted to incorporate portions of the Bill of Rights into the State constitutions—for example prohibiting the establishment of State churches—but this was rejected. As with the other amendments in the Bill of Rights, the intent of the First is easy to ascertain and only made cloudy by silver-tongued lawyers and judges bent on political gain.

The first liberty protected by the First Amendment, "freedom of religion," has received the most attention. What did the Founders mean by the "establishment of religion"? The Virginia and North Carolina proposals made clear their definition. "No particular religious sect or society ought to be favored or established, by law, in preference to others."[16] In other words, the Congress would not be able to legally establish a "religious sect or society"— that is, a specific Christian denomination—as the "Church of the

United States" in the manner of the established Church of England. But this did not by any means imply that the Founders intended public life to be devoid of religion.

Amos Singletary said in the Massachusetts Ratifying Convention that he was troubled that "there was no provision that men in power should have any *religion*; and though he hoped to see Christians, yet by the Constitution, a Papist, or an Infidel, was as eligible as they...in this instance, we were giving great power to we know not whom." Thomas Lusk lamented in the same convention that "Roman Catholics, Papists, and Pagans might be introduced into office, and that Popery and the Inquisition may be established in America." Isaac Backus, a leading proponent of freedom of conscience in colonial America, answered that because the Constitution forbade religious tests (Article VI, Clause 3), "Popery, or some other tyrannical way of worship..." could not be established by the Congress. Daniel Shute, however, provided the clearest explanation of the word "religion." "Far from limiting my charity and confidence to men of my own denomination in religion, I suppose, and I believe, sir, that there are worthy characters among men of every denomination—among Quakers, the Baptists, the Church of England, the Papists; and even among those who have no other guide, in the way of virtue and heaven, than the dictates of natural religion."[17]

Virginia and North Carolina were the two States that proposed an amendment guaranteeing religious freedom, so their views might deserve special weight. In North Carolina, Henry Abbot equated "*religion*" with denomination. "I believe the majority of the community are Presbyterians. I am, for my part, against any exclusive establishment; but if there were any, I would prefer the Episcopal." North Carolina's governor Samuel Johnston defined "religion" the same way and commented that the "religions" of the States included members of the Presbyterian, Baptist, and Episcopalian churches, as well as Quakers and other "sects." Some members of the Convention used the word "religion" in its broader sense. But there was unanimity that morality and religion were bedrocks of a stable society.[18]

Madison made the most revealing statement in regard to the *intent* of the "establishment clause" during debate over the amendment in 1789. He proposed that the word "national" be inserted before "religion." This would, he hoped, "satisfy the minds of honorable gentlemen. He believed that the people feared one sect might obtain a pre-eminence, or two combine together, and establish a religion to which they would compel others to conform. He thought if the word national was introduced, it would point the amendment directly to the object it was intended to prevent."[19] For Madison, the purpose was to prevent the establishment of a national "Church of the United States." In no way was it to inhibit the constitutionally protected "free exercise" of religion. And again, the First Amendment applied only to the *general* government. States had free rein on this issue, and most had either an established church or a strict religious test for office holders.[20]

The other liberties in the First Amendment, freedom of speech and the press, the right to petition the government, and the right to assemble, faced little debate, and were considered essential for a free people, particularly freedom of the press. Arthur Lee, writing as "Cincinnatus" to James Wilson in 1787, said, "I have proved, sir, that not only some power is given in the constitution to restrain, and even to subject the press, but that it is a power totally unlimited; and may certainly annihilate the freedom of the press, and convert it from being the palladium of liberty to become an engine of imposition and tyranny. It is an easy step from restraining the press to making it place the worst actions of government in so favorable a light, that we may groan under tyranny and oppression without knowing from whence it comes."[21] Richard Henry Lee wrote that "a free press is the channel of communication as to mercantile and public affairs; by means of it the people in large countries ascertain each others' sentiments; are enabled to unite, and become formidable to those rulers who adopt improper measures. Newspapers may sometimes be the vehicles of abuse, and of many things not true; but these are but small inconveniences, in my mind, among many advantages."[22]

A free press was essential in the time leading to the American War for Independence. The founding generation argued that it kept government honest or at the very least exposed political transgressions. This is why Jefferson and Madison, through the Virginia and Kentucky Resolutions, vehemently opposed the Sedition Law of 1798 as a violation of the First Amendment. The Sedition Law of 1798 showed that even men in the founding generation were prone to support unwise and unconstitutional legislation in a time of stress (in this case a potential war with France). That is precisely why the First Amendment was proposed and ratified and why it should be jealously guarded.

"The right of the people to be secure in their persons, houses, papers, and effects, against unreasonable searches and seizures, shall not be violated, and no Warrants shall issue, but upon probable cause, supported by Oath or affirmation, and particularly describing the place to be searched, and the persons or things to be seized." **Amendment IV.**

"No person shall be held to answer for a capital, or otherwise infamous crime, unless on a presentment or indictment of a Grand Jury, except in cases arising in the land or naval forces, or in the Militia, when in actual service in time of War or public danger; nor shall any person be subject for the same offence to be twice put in jeopardy of life or limb; nor shall be compelled in any criminal case to be a witness against himself, nor be deprived of life, liberty, or property, without due process of law; nor shall private property be taken for public use, without just compensation." **Amendment V.**

"In all criminal prosecutions, the accused shall enjoy the right to a speedy and public trial, by an impartial jury of the State and district wherein the crime shall have been committed, which district shall have been previously ascertained by law, and to be informed of the nature and cause of the accusation; to be confronted with the witnesses against him; to have compulsory process for obtaining witnesses in his favor, and to have the Assistance of Counsel for his defence." **Amendment VI.**

"In Suits at common law, where the value in controversy shall exceed twenty dollars, the right of trial by jury shall be preserved, and no fact tried by a jury, shall be otherwise re-examined in any Court of the United States, than according to the rules of the common law." **Amendment VII.**

"Excessive bail shall not be required, nor excessive fines imposed, nor cruel and unusual punishments inflicted."
Amendment VIII.

Amendments IV–VIII were designed to protect the lives, liberty, and property of the people. All restricted the judicial power of the United States government and were intended to quiet one of the main criticisms of the Constitution, namely that the Constitution did not define trial by jury or protect the rights of the accused. Opponents hammered on this issue during the ratification debates. State constitutions, of course, typically outlined these essential liberties in their respective declarations of rights, but because the federal court system, namely the Supreme Court, was to have jurisdiction "both as to Law and Fact," and because Congress could establish inferior tribunals (which they argued would destroy the State court systems), opponents of the Constitution argued that they would trample the rights of the people.

Abraham Holmes made a lengthy speech on these issues in the Massachusetts Ratifying Convention. He argued, "On the whole, when we fully consider this matter, and fully investigate the powers granted, explicitly given, and specially delegated, we shall find Congress possessed of powers enabling them to institute judicatories little less inauspicious than a certain tribunal in Spain, which has long been the disgrace of Christendom: I mean that diabolical institution, the *Inquisition*." Plus, Congress, he said, was "nowhere restrained from inventing the most cruel and unheard-of punishments, and annexing them to crimes; and there is no constitutional check on them, but that *racks* and *gibbets* may be amongst the most mild instruments of their discipline." If this did not happen, Holmes said it would be "owning *entirely*...to the goodness of the men, and not in the *least degree* owning to the goodness of the Constitution."[23]

He wasn't alone. The dissenting minority in Pennsylvania wrote that "the loss of the invaluable right of trial by an unbiased jury, so dear to every friend of liberty, the monstrous experience and inconveniences of the mode of proceeding to be adopted, are such as will prove intolerable to the people of this country."[24] George Mason made this one of his principle objections to the Constitution. Richard Henry Lee said that "it is essential in every free country, that common people should have a part and share of influence, in the judicial as well as in the legislative department."[25] Luther Martin railed that "*jury trials*, which have ever been the *boast* of the English constitution, which have been by our several *State constitutions* so *cautiously secured* to us,—*jury trials* which have so long been considered the *surest barrier* against *arbitrary power*, and the *palladium* of *liberty*,—with the *loss* of *which* the *loss* of our *freedom* may be dated, are *taken* away by the proposed form of government, not *only* in a *great variety of questions between individual* and *individual*, but in *every case* whether *civil* or *criminal* arising *under the laws of* the United States or the *execution* of those laws...."[26]

Alexander Hamilton reasoned in Federalist No. 83 that "it certainly sounds not a little harsh and extraordinary to affirm that there is no security for liberty in a constitution which expressly establishes the trial by jury in criminal cases, because it does not do it in civil also...."[27] James Iredell, in the North Carolina Ratifying Convention, noted that though the Constitution did not "provide expressly for a trial by jury in civil cases, it does not say that there shall not be such a trial." And, he reminded the delegates, "The greatest danger from ambition is in criminal cases. But here they have no option. The trial must be by jury, in the state wherein the offense is committed; and the writ of *habeas corpus* will in the mean time secure the citizen against arbitrary imprisonment, which has been the principal source of tyranny in all ages."[28]

The logical question to ask is why the majority of the founding generation considered trial by jury to be an essential liberty. The answer is "jury nullification," a practice dating back to seventeenth-century England, allowing a jury to void an unconstitutional or otherwise "bad" law through its verdict. Such "jury nullification" was considered an important check against despotic government. Juries, composed of an "impartial" people "of the State and district wherein the crime shall have been committed" typically allowed the "common people," as Richard Henry Lee called them, the ability to check the potentially arbitrary power of judges; bad and unpopular laws were often disregarded by juries; and the Eighth Amendment against excessive bails and fines and cruel and unusual punishment tied judges' hands in regard to sentencing.

As for property, the Fourth and Fifth Amendments curtailed the ability of the general government to "search and seize" property without "due process," meaning they have to follow proper legal procedures. This was born from the American War for Independence. During the 1760s, the British government issued writs of assistance—a legal order authorizing a sheriff or other public official to search private property. They were highly unpopular, often arbitrary, and eventually illegal, but the Constitution, without the Bill of Rights, did not prevent their resurrection in America. The delegates to the Maryland Ratification Convention argued that without the Fourth Amendment, "our dwelling houses, those castles considered so sacred by the English law, will be laid open to the insolence and oppression of office...."[29] Private property is also protected under the Fifth Amendment, which states that an individual whose private property is taken for public use must be justly compensated.

> "A well regulated Militia, being necessary to the security of a free State, the right of the people to keep and bear Arms, shall not be infringed." **Amendment II.**

> "No Soldier shall, in time of peace be quartered in any house, without the consent of the Owner, nor in time of war, but in a manner to be prescribed by law." **Amendment III.**

The Second and Third Amendments to the Constitution were intended to reassure those who feared federal control of the militia and a possible permanent standing army. As per Article I, Section 8, Clause 16, the general government has the power to arm the militia of the several States. Opponents of this power argued that if the general government could arm the militia, it could also *refuse* to arm it as well, thus leaving the people unable to defend themselves.

Both North Carolina and Virginia proposed that "the people have a right to keep and bear arms; that a well-regulated militia, composed of the body of the people trained in arms, is the proper, natural, and safe defense of a free state; that standing armies, in time of peace, are dangerous to liberty, and therefore ought to be avoided...."[30] Pennsylvania's proposal read, "That the people have a right to bear arms *for the defense of themselves and their own state, or the United States,* or for the purpose of killing game; and no law shall be passed for disarming the people or any of them, unless for crimes committed, or real danger of public injury from individuals...."[31] Melancton Smith offered the following at the New York Ratifying Convention, "that the [general government's] powers to organize, arm, and discipline the militia, shall not be construed to extend further than to prescribe the mode of arming and disciplining the same."[32]

Maryland did not propose an amendment that resembled the Second, but it did provide a definition of the militia as "all men, able to bear arms." As such, Maryland wanted the militia to be subject to martial law only "in time of war, invasion, or rebellion."[33] George Mason said in the Virginia Ratifying Convention that the militia "consist now of the whole people, except a few public officers."[34] Hence, the militia was everyone, "composed of the body of people trained in arms," not the modern "National Guard." It was designed to render a standing army unnecessary, and to do so every man had to be armed for the "defense of themselves and their own state, or the United States," as Pennsylvania contended.

When the amendment was up for debate in the House in 1789, no one questioned its intent. In fact, Elbridge Gerry made his understanding of the amendment quite clear. "What, sir, is the use of a militia? It is to prevent the establishment of a standing army, the bane of liberty.... Whenever Governments mean to invade the rights and liberties of the people, they always attempt to destroy the militia, in order to raise an army upon their ruins." The only significant disagreement that took place over the Second Amendment was whether there should be a "conscientious objector clause" to allow those with "religious scruples" to avoid bearing arms. The clause was ultimately rejected, making all men eligible for service in the militia unless otherwise regulated by State law.

The Third Amendment was another guard against the potential for an oppressive standing army. During the time leading to the American War for Independence, the British, through the Quartering Acts, required colonists to provide barracks and supplies for British soldiers. By 1774, British troops could, by law, be stationed in the homes of private citizens, which might have been tolerable in a war such as the French and Indian War, but was utterly intolerable and oppressive in a time of peace. Patrick Henry said in the Virginia Ratifying Convention that "one of our first complaints, under the former government, was the quartering of troops upon us. This was one of the principal reasons for dissolving the connection with Great Britain. Here we may have troops in time of peace. They may be billeted in any manner—to tyrannize, oppress, and crush us."[35]

Thomas Sumter, the "Fighting Gamecock" of South Carolina and a hero of the American War for Independence, remarked in 1789 that he "hoped soldiers would never be quartered on the inhabitants, either in time of peace or war, without the consent of the owner. It was a burden, and very oppressive, even in cases where the owner gave his consent; but where this was wanting, it would be a hardship indeed! Their property would lie at the mercy of men irritated by a refusal, and well disposed to destroy the peace of the family."[36] He would have known better than most. His State suffered under the heel of the British army during the War. (It was partly because of his daring tactics that Lord Charles Cornwallis was forced out of the State and into Virginia in 1781.)

Several States proposed amendments that would have prohibited a standing army. All were either rejected in the State conventions or never made it past Madison. Yet, this did not mean that the founding generation indiscriminately approved of a standing army. Madison said that a militia was the best security against one, and with the Second and Third Amendments, most men in the founding generation believed the right of the people to resist tyrannical government was secure. They typically argued a standing army could be useful, but that the preference should be for the people to defend themselves through their State militias.

In Federalist No. 43, James Madison praised the amendment procedure in Article V of the Constitution. "The mode preferred by the Convention seems to be stamped with every mark of propriety. It guards equally against that extreme facility which would render the Constitution too mutable; and that extreme difficulty which might perpetuate its discovered faults. It moreover equally enables the general and the state governments to originate the amendment of errors as they may be pointed out by the experience on one side or on the other."[37] James Iredell declared in the North Carolina Ratifying Convention that "this, indeed, is one of the greatest beauties of the system, and should strongly recommend it to every candid mind. The Constitution of any government which cannot be regularly amended when its defects are experienced, reduces the people to this dilemma—they must either submit to its oppressions, or bring about amendments, more or less, by a civil war."[38] Madison's argument has generally been used as the primary defense of the amendment process. No one argued that the Constitution should be so easy to amend as to make it a worthless scrap of paper, but several thought it would be too hard and therefore would saddle the American people with a despotic government.

Patrick Henry was outraged over the supermajority it required to amend the Constitution. "A trifling minority may reject the most salutary amendments. Is this an easy mode of securing the public liberty? It is, sir, a most fearful situation, when the most contemptible minority can prevent the alteration of the most oppressive government; for it may, in many respects, prove to be such. Is this the spirit of republicanism?"[39] George Bryan of Pennsylvania, writing as "An Old Whig," had a dire prediction should an un-amended Constitution be ratified. "Inveterate power is at all times very hard to be controuled. Habits, connexions, dependence, and a thousand circumstances in a course of time, rivet the chains of slavery "till we grow either callous to their galling, or too feeble to shake them off, or too listless to resist. Ask the beaten Turk to resume his liberty, or the tired horse to resume his pristine freedom.—As well you might ask the galled sons of America, a few years hence, to assert the native rights of men, if the proposed constitution be once fixed upon us. It will be extremely difficult to change it for the better even in the beginning; but in a little time it will become utterly impossible."[40]

The founding generation adopted twelve amendments to the Constitution. It has only been amended fifteen times since, and one of those amendments, the Twenty-seventh—"No law, varying the compensation for the services of the Senators and Representatives, shall take effect, until an election of Representatives shall have intervened"—was initially part of the proposed Bill of Rights. The Constitution has proved to be difficult to amend, maybe too difficult. Americans today are generally uninterested in constitutional amendments, though perhaps the currently debated "balanced budget amendment" will show that Americans have not become "too listless to resist" the massive power of the general government.

Whose Constitution?

Conservatives generally claim to be strict constructionists and view the Constitution as a "limiting document" on federal power. Liberals usually see the Constitution as a "living document" that grants expansive powers to the general government through its broad "sweeping clauses." In truth, both sides are right, to a degree, but conservatives have a better claim on the Constitution *as ratified*, particularly with the inclusion of the Bill of Rights in 1791.

Liberals typically interpret the Constitution as its opponents *warned* it would be read. When liberals trumpet the "General Welfare Clause," the "Necessary and Proper Clause," or the "Supremacy Clause" as a rationale for centralizing power in the general government, they are vindicating the fears of the Constitution's opponents in 1787 and 1788. But this does not mean they interpret the Constitution correctly. On the contrary, they interpret the Constitution in a way that the document's original supporters said it *should not be* interpreted. The Constitution is not a "limiting document," in the sense that it gave the general government far more power than it had under the Articles of Confederation; but the general government's authority was to be limited by its enumerated constitutional powers. Liberals have relentlessly expanded these powers without amending the Constitution, simply by playing on the American public's ignorance of how the Constitution was written and ratified, as well as what it means.

The Constitution *as ratified* can be summarized in a few points:

- The Constitution is not intended to consolidate or abolish the States. There were members of both the Philadelphia Convention and the State ratifying conventions who wanted that to happen (they hid their intentions well during the ratification debates), but proponents of the final draft sold it to the States on the basis that the States retained most of their sovereignty.

- The document is supposed to be limited by its delegated powers. As nationalists James Wilson, Alexander Hamilton, and several others argued during the ratification process, those powers not granted to the government were reserved to the people and the States.

- Most of the Constitution's former opponents thought that the addition of the Bill of Rights—especially the Tenth Amendment—would provide the necessary check on central power.

- The executive does not have the powers of a king, and judges cannot rule on State laws clearly outside of their jurisdiction (as most are).

- The Constitution is a compact among the people of the States, not the amorphous "people of the United States." The ratification process clearly illustrates that point.

Opponents of the Constitution were often right about how the Constitution would be abused. Yet, if the Constitution was consistently interpreted *as ratified*, there would be no reason to fear the general government. The problem is that neither major American political party adheres to that Constitution; many of our elected representatives are ignorant of its text and original meaning. The only hope lies in a better educated public. Americans do not need judges, lawyers, politicians, or ivory tower academics descending to provide answers to our constitutional questions. The Founding Fathers have already done that for us. We just need to read what they said and hold politicians in Washington accountable.

Appendix A

The quotations used in the preceding text are only a small sample of the many volumes of public pronouncements concerning the proposed Constitution in 1787 and 1788. Below are several others that did not make it into the narrative but that could have readily been used in place of the selections I chose for the primary text. Knowing that they could have been part of a larger stand-alone volume, these quotations are provided to further whet the reader's appetite.

The Founders on Consolidation of the States

- "It is the opinion of the greatest writers, that a very extensive country cannot be governed on democratical principles, on any other plan, than a confederation of a number of small republics, possessing all the powers of internal government, but united in the management of their foreign and general concerns. It would not be difficult to prove, that anything short of despotism could not bind so great a country under one government; and that whatever plan you might, at the first setting out, establish, it would issue in a despotism." **George Bryan of Pennsylvania, 1787**[1]

- "We cannot have a limited monarchy... our situation will not allow it—Repubs. are for a while industrious but finally destroy [the]mselves—they were badly constituted—I dread a Consolidation of the States." **John Dickinson of Delaware, 1787**[2]

- "Any law... of the United States, for securing to Congress more than a concurrent right with each state, is usurpation, and void." **Theophilus Parsons of Massachusetts, 1788**[3]

- "If the gentleman will attend, he will see this is a government for confederated states; that, consequently, it can never intermeddle where no power is given." **Archibald Maclaine of North Carolina, 1788**[4]

- "Mr. Chairman, if they mean, *We the people,*—the people at large,—I conceive the expression is improper. Were not they who framed this Constitution the representatives of the legislatures of the different states? In my opinion, they had no power, from the people at large, to use their name, or to act for them. They were not delegated for that purpose." **David Caldwell of North Carolina, 1788**[5]
- "If there were any seeds in this Constitution which might, one day, produce a consolidation, it would, sir, with me, be an insuperable objection, I am so perfectly convinced that so extensive a country as this can never be managed by one consolidated government.... If the state governments vanish, the general government must vanish also.... The state governments can put a *veto*, at any time, on the general government, by ceasing to continue the executive power." **William Richardson Davie of North Carolina, 1788**[6]
- "The treaty of peace [Treaty of Paris 1783] expressly agreed to acknowledge us as free, sovereign, and independent states, which privileges we lived at present in the exercise of. But this new Constitution at once swept those privileges away, being sovereign over all; so that this state would dwindle into a mere skeleton of what it was; its legislative powers would be pared down to little more than those now vested in the corporation; and he should value the honor of a seat in the legislature in no higher esteem than

a seat in the city council." **Rawlins Lowndes of South Carolina, 1788**[7]

- "What does this proposed Constitution do? It changes, totally changes, the form of your present government. What have you been contending for these ten years past? Liberty! What is liberty? The power of governing yourselves. If you adopt this Constitution, have you this power? No: you give it into the hands of a set of men who live one thousand miles distant from you. Let the people but once trust their liberties out of their own hands, and what will be the consequence? First, a haughty, imperious aristocracy; and ultimately, a tyrannical monarchy." **James Lincoln of South Carolina, 1788**[8]

- "The quoting of ancient history was no more to the purpose than to tell how our forefathers dug clams at Plymouth; he feared a *consolidation* of the thirteen states. Our manners, he said, were widely different from the Southern States; their elections were not so *free and unbiased*; therefore, if the states were consolidated, he thought it would introduce manners among us which would set us at continual variance." **Benjamin Randall of Massachusetts, 1788**[9]

- "It has been observed, that, as the people must, of necessity, delegate essential powers either to the individual or general sovereignties, it is perfectly immaterial where they are lodged; but, as the state

governments will always possess a better representation of the feelings and interests of the people at
large, it is obvious that those powers can be depos-
ited with much greater safety with the state than
the general government... [and] a consolidated
government, partaking in a great degree of republican principles, and which had in object the control of the inhabitants of the extensive territory of
the United States, by its sole operations, could not
preserve the essential rights and liberties of the
people." **John Lansing of New York, 1788**[10]

- "Thus, early in the debate, the honorable gentleman
had himself shown that the intent of the Constitution was not a confederacy, but a reduction of all the
states into a consolidated government. He hoped
the gentleman would be complaisant enough to
exchange names with those who disliked the Constitution, as it appeared from his own concessions,
that they were federalists, and those who advocated
it were anti-federalists." **Melancton Smith of New
York, 1788**[11]

- "The state governments possess inherent advantages, which will ever give them an influence and
ascendency over the national government, and will
forever preclude the possibility of federal encroachments. That their liberties, indeed, can be subverted
by the federal head, is repugnant to every rule of
political calculation." **Alexander Hamilton of New
York, 1788**[12]

- "The constitution should be so formed as not to swallow up the state governments: the general government ought to be confined to national objects; and the states should retain such powers as concern their own internal police." **John Williams of New York, 1788**[13]

- "Congress can no more abolish the state governments, than they can dissolve the Union. The whole Constitution is repugnant to it...." **Alexander Hamilton of New York, 1788**[14]

- "Sir, I contemplate the abolition of the *state constitutions* as an event fatal to the liberties of America.... In a country where a portion of the people lives more than twelve hundred miles from the centre [*sic*], I think that one body cannot possibly legislate for the whole." **Melancton Smith of New York, 1788**[15]

- "Sir, if you do not give the state governments a power to protect themselves, if you leave them no other check upon Congress than the power of appointing senators, they will certainly be overcome...." **John Lansing of New York, 1788**

- "Is it to be supposed that one national government will suit so extensive a country, embracing so many climates, and containing inhabitants so very different in manners, habits, and customs? It is ascertained, by history, that there never was a government over a very extensive country without destroying the liberties of the people: history also, supported by the opinions of the best writers, shows us that monarchy may suit a large territory, and despotic governments ever so extensive a country, but that popular governments can only exist in small territories. Is there a single example, on the face of the earth, to support a contrary opinion? Where is there one exception to this general rule? Was there ever an instance of a general national government extending over so extensive a country, abounding in such a variety of climates, &c., where the people retained their liberty?" **George Mason of Virginia, 1788**[16]

- "If this be such a government [consolidated], I will confess, with my worthy friend, that it is inadmissible over such a territory as this country. Let us consider whether it be such a government or not. I should understand a consolidated government to be that which should have the sole and exclusive power, legislative, executive, and judicial, without any limitation. Is this such a government? Or can it be changed to such a one? It only extends to the general purposes of the Union. It does not intermeddle with the local, particular affairs of the states." **Edmund Pendleton of Virginia, 1788**[17]

- "We are told that this government, collectively taken, is without an example; that it is national in this part, and federal in that part, &c. We may be amused, if we please, by a treatise of political anatomy. In the brain it is national; the stamina are federal; some limbs are federal, others national. The senators are voted for by the state legislatures; so far it is federal. Individuals choose the members of the first branch; here it is national. It is federal conferring general powers, but national in retaining them. It is not to be supported by the states; the pockets of individuals are to be searched for its maintenance. What signifies it to me that you have the most curious anatomical description of it in its creation? To all the common purposes of legislation, it is a great consolidation of government." **Patrick Henry of Virginia, 1788**[18]

• "If this were a consolidated government, ought it not to be ratified by a majority of the people as individuals, and not as states? Suppose Virginia, Connecticut, Massachusetts, and Pennsylvania, had ratified it; these four states, being a majority of the people of America, would, by their adoption, have made it binding on all the states, had this been a consolidated government. But it is only the government of those seven states who have adopted it." **Henry Lee of Virginia, 1788**[19]

The Founders on a Bicameral Legislature, Democracy, and the States

• "The people...should have as little to do as may be about the government. They want information, and are consistently liable to be misled." **Roger Sherman of Connecticut, 1787**[20]

• "[The House of Representatives ought] to be the grand depository of the democratic principle of the government.... We have been too democratic, but [I am] afraid we should incautiously run into the opposite extreme. We ought to attend to the rights of every class of the people." **George Mason of Virginia, 1787**[21]

- "The popular election of one branch of the national legislature [is] essential to every plan of free government." **James Madison of Virginia, 1787**[22]

- "It [is] essential that one branch of the legislature should be drawn immediately from the people, and expedient that the other should be chosen by the legislatures of the states. This combination of the state governments with the national government was as politic as it was unavoidable." **John Dickinson of Delaware, 1787**[23]

- "[I am] for an election by the people as to the first branch, and by the states as to the second branch; by which means the citizens of the states would be represented both *individually* and *collectively*." **William Pierce of Georgia, 1787**[24]

- "[I want] domestic happiness. The national government could not descend to the local objects on which this depended. It could only embrace objects of a general nature. [I turn] my eyes, therefore, for the preservation of his rights to the state governments. From these alone he could derive the greatest happiness he expects in this life. [My] happiness depends on their existence, as much as a new-born infant on its mother for nourishment." **Oliver Ellsworth of Connecticut, 1787**[25]

- "The Constitution effectually secures the states in their several rights. It must secure them for its own sake; for they are the pillars which uphold the general system. The Senate, a constituent branch of the general legislature, without whose assent no public act can be made, are appointed by the states, and will secure the rights of the several states. The other branch of the legislature, the Representatives, are to be elected by the people at large. They will therefore be the guardians of the rights of the great body of the citizens. So well guarded is this Constitution throughout, that it seems impossible that the rights of either of the states or of the people should be destroyed." **Oliver Wolcott of Connecticut, 1788**[26]

- "It has pleased Heaven to afford the United States means for the attainment of this great object [peace], which it has withheld from other nations. They speak the same language; they profess the same religion; and what is of infinitely more importance, they acknowledge the same great principle of government—a principle, if not unknown, at least little understood in the old world—*that all power is derived from the people*. They consider the state and the general government as different deposits of that power. In this view, it is of little moment to them whether that portion of it which they must, for their own happiness, lodge in their rulers, be invested in the state governments only, or shared between them and the councils of Union. The rights they reserve are not diminished, and

probably their liberty acquires an additional security from the division." **Robert R. Livingston of
New York, 1788**[27]

- "After much anxious discussion…a compromise
was effected, by which it was determined that the
first branch be so chosen as to represent in due
proportion the people of the Union; that the Senate
should be the representatives of the states, where
each should have an equal weight." **Charles
Pinckney of South Carolina, 1788**[28]

- "If great affairs of government were trusted to few
men, they would be more liable to corruption. Corruption, he knew, was unfashionable amongst us,
but he supposed that Americans were like any other
men; and though they had hitherto displayed great
virtues, still they were men; and therefore such steps
should be taken as to prevent the possibility of corruption." **Melancton Smith of New York, 1788**[29]

- "I conceive the state governments are necessary as
the barrier between the people's liberties and any
invasion which may be attempted on them by the
general government." **Gilbert Livingston of New
York, 1788**[30]

- "With respect to the representation so much
applauded, I cannot think it such a full and free one
as it is represented; but I must candidly acknowledge that this defect results from the very nature of
the government. It would be impossible to have a
full and adequate representation in the general
government; it would be too expensive and too

unwieldy. We are, then, under the necessity of having this a very inadequate representation. Is this general representation to be compared with the real, actual, substantial representation of the state legislatures? It cannot bear a comparison. To make representation real and actual, the number of representatives ought to be adequate; they ought to mix with the people, think as they think, feel as they feel,—ought to be perfectly amenable to them, and thoroughly acquainted with their interest and condition." **George Mason of Virginia, 1788**[31]

- "It is impiously irritating the avenging hand of Heaven, when a people, who are in the full enjoyment of freedom, launch out into the wide ocean of human affairs, and desert those maxims which alone can preserve liberty. Such maxims, humble as they are, are those only which can render a nation safe or formidable." **Patrick Henry of Virginia, 1788**[32]

The Founders on Term Length and Term Limits

- "The more *frequent* elections are, the oftener states will be exposed to be deprived of their voice and influence in the national councils. I think annual elections are too short for so extensive an empire. They keep the members always traveling about; and I am of opinion that elections for two years are in no way subversive of the liberties of the *people*." **Francis Dana of Massachusetts, 1788**[33]

- "I am opposed to biennial, and am in favor of annual elections. Annual elections have been the practice of this state ever since its settlement, and no objection to such a mode of electing has ever been made. It has, indeed, sir, been considered as the safeguard of the liberties of the people; and the annihilation of it, the avenue through which tyranny will enter." **Dr. John Taylor of Massachusetts, 1788**[34]

- "It is admitted that annual elections may be highly fit for the state legislature. Every citizen grows up with a knowledge of the local circumstances of the state. But the business of the federal government will be very different. The objects of their power are few and national. At least two years in office will be necessary to enable a man to judge of the trade and interests of the state which he never saw. The time, I hope, will come, when this excellent country will furnish food, and freedom, (which is better than food, which is the food of the soul,) for fifty millions of happy people. Will any man say that the national business can be understood in one year?" **Fisher Ames of Massachusetts, 1788**[35]

- "The senators are to serve six years. This is only two years longer than the senators of this state hold their places. One third of the members are to go out every two years; and in six, the whole body will be changed. Prior to the revolution, the representatives in the several colonies were elected for different periods—for three years, for seven years, &c. Were those bodies ever considered as incapable of representing the people, or as too independent of them?" **Alexander Hamilton of New York, 1788**[36]

- "We have generally found that perpetual bodies have either combined in some scheme of usurpation, or have been torn and distracted with cabals. Both have been the source of misfortunes to the state. Most people acquainted with history will acknowledge these facts. Our Congress would have been a fine field for party spirit to act in. That body would undoubtedly have suffered all the evils of faction, had it not been secured by the rotation established by the Articles of Confederation. I think a *rotation* in the government is a very important and truly republican institution. All good republicans, I presume to say, will treat it with respect." **Melancton Smith of New York, 1788**[37]

- "It is strange to mark, however, what a sudden and striking revolution has taken place in the political sentiments of America, for, sir, in the opening of our struggle with Great Britain, it was often insisted that annual parliaments were necessary to secure the liberties of the people, and yet it is here proposed to establish a House of Representatives which shall continue for two, a Senate for six, and a President for four years! What is there in this plan indeed, which can even assure us that the several departments shall continue no longer in office?" **Robert Whitehill of Pennsylvania, 1787**[38]

- "If one year be not too long to elect a State Representative, give me leave to say, that two years ought not to be considered too long for the election of members of the general Legislature. The objects of the former are narrow and limited to State and local affairs—the objects of the latter are co-extensive with the continent." **George Nicholas of Virginia, 1788**[39]

- "I would have preferred annual elections of the delegates, but do not conceive we are unsafe because they are biennial—the house of burgesses under the old government, though they held their seats at the pleasure of the crown were always patriotic—and the commons of England whose elections are septenial [*sic*], never attempted such direful things as are foretold of Congress." **Alexander White of Virginia, 1787**[40]

The Founders on the Senate

- "The state governments are essential parts of the system, and the defence [*sic*] of this article is drawn from its tendency to their preservation. The senators represent the sovereignty of the states.... If they would be brought by that means [direct election] more immediately under the influence of the people, then they will represent the state legislatures less, and become the representatives of individuals.... This would totally obliterate the federal features of the Constitution. What would become of the state governments, and on whom would devolve the duty of defending them against the

encroachments of the federal government? A consolidation of the states would ensue, which, it is
conceded, would subvert the new Constitution, and
against which this very article, so much con-
demned, is our best security. Too much provision
cannot be made against confederation. *The state
governments represent the wishes, and feelings, and
local interests, of the people. They are the safeguard
and ornament of the Constitution; they will protract
the period of our liberties; they will afford a shelter
against the abuse of power, and will be the natural
avengers of our violated rights*" (emphasis added).
Fisher Ames of Massachusetts, 1788[41]

- "This great source of free government, popular
election, should be perfectly pure, and the most
unbounded liberty allowed. Where this principle is
adhered to; where, in the organization of the government, the legislative, executive, and judicial
branches are rendered distinct; where, again, the
legislature is divided into separate houses, and the
operations of each are controlled by various checks
and balances, and, *above all, by the vigilance and
weight of the state governments* (the Senate)—to talk
of tyranny, and the subversion of our liberties, is to
speak the language of enthusiasm" (emphasis
added). **Alexander Hamilton of New York, 1788**[42]

- "The Senate is to be composed of men appointed
by the state legislatures: they will certainly choose
those who are most distinguished for their general
knowledge. I presume they will also instruct them,

that there will be a constant correspondence supported between the senators and the state executives, who will be able, from time to time, to afford them all that particular information which particular circumstances may require." **John Jay of New York, 1788**[43]

- "I believe it was undoubtedly the intention of the framers of this Constitution to make the lower house the proper, peculiar representative of the interests of the people; the Senate, of the sovereignty of the states." **John Lansing of New York, 1788**[44]

- "As the Constitution now stands, I see no possible danger of the senators' losing their attachment to the states...." **Richard Harrison of New York, 1788**[45]

- "As the Senate represents the sovereignty of the states, whatever might affect the states in the political capacity ought to be left to them. This is the certain means of preventing a consolidation.... I had the honor to observe to the committee, before, the causes of the particular formation of the Senate—that it was owing, with other reason, to the *jealousy* of the states, and, particularly, to the extreme jealousy of the lesser states of the power and influence of the larger members of the confederacy. It was in the Senate that the several political interests of the states were to be preserved, and where all their powers were to be perfectly balanced." **William Richardson Davie of North Carolina, 1788**[46]

- "It seems to be forgotten that the Senate is placed there for a very valuable purpose—as a guard against any attempt of consolidation.... Thus, then, the general government is to be taken care of, and the state governments to be preserved. The former is done by a numerous representation of the people of each state, in proportion to its importance. The latter is effected by giving each state an equal representation in the Senate. The people will be represented in one house, the state legislatures in the other." **James Iredell of North Carolina, 1788**[47]

- "The twenty-six Senators, Representatives of the States, will not be those desperadoes and horrid adventurers which they are represented to be. The State Legislatures, I trust, will not forget the duty they owe to their country so far, as to choose such men to manage their federal interests." **Edmund Randolph of Virginia, 1788**[48]

The Founders on Corporations and Monopolies and Commerce

- "Mr. Gerry's objections.... The Power given respectg. [*sic*] Commerce will enable the Legislature to create corporations and monopolies." **Elbridge Gerry of Massachusetts on his refusal to sign the Constitution, 1787**[49]
- "Under their own construction of the general clause at the end of the enumerated powers [Necessary and Proper Clause], the Congress may grant monopolies in trade and commerce...." **George Mason of Virginia on his refusal to sign the Constitution, 1787**[50]

- "By sect. 8 of article 1. Congress are to have the unlimited right to regulate commerce, external and *internal*, and may therefore create monopolies which have been universally injurious to all the subjects of the countries that have adopted them, excepting the monopolies themselves." **James Winthrop of Massachusetts, 1788**[51]

- "It is not probable that the national legislature will be so impolitic as to make any laws whereby the inter[e]st of one part of the community can be sacrificed to the advantages of the other;—and in the next place, allowing that they will pass an act to prohibit foreigners from being the carriers of our produce, it will by no means follow that the Northern States will demand an exorbitant freight." **Tobias Lear of Virginia, 1787**[52]

- "The power of regulating commerce by a bare majority and that of taxing will ruin the Southern States...." **William Grayson of Virginia, 1787**[53]

- "By requiring only a majority to make all commercial and navigation laws, the five Southern States will be ruined; for such rigid and premature regulations may be made, as will enable the merchants of the northern and eastern States not only to demand an exorbitant freight, but to monopolize the purchase of the commodities at their own price, for many years...." **George Mason of Virginia, 1787**[54]

- "Like thirteen contentious neighbours [*sic*] we devour and take every advantage of each other, and are without that system of policy which gives safety and strength, and constitutes a national structure. Once we were dependant [sic] only on Great-Britain, now we are dependant [sic] on every petty state in the world and on every custom house officer of foreign ports. If the injured apply for redress to the assemblies of the several states, it is in vain, for they are not, and cannot be known abroad. If they apply to Congress, it is also vain, for however wise and good that body may be, they have not power to vindicate either themselves or their subjects.... You are oppressed for a want of power which can protect commerce, encourage business, and create a ready demand for the productions of your farms." **Oliver Ellsworth of Connecticut, 1787**[55]

- "An unrestricted intercourse between the States themselves will advance the trade of each, by an interchange of their respective productions, not only for the supply of reciprocal wants at home, but for exportation to foreign markets." **Alexander Hamilton of New York, 1787**[56]

- "The want of a qualified Navigation Act, is already declared to be a means by which the produce of the Southern States will be reduced to nothing, & will become a monopoly of the Northern & Eastern States...." **George Washington of Virginia, 1787**[57]

- "We shall derive prodigious Advantages from the Regulation of our Trade with foreign Powers who have taken the Opportunity of our feeble State to turn everything to their own Benefit—by playing off one Nation against another we may bring them

one after the other to some Consideration for us,
wh [*sic*] they have not had for some Years past—
They have sacrificed our Interest in every Instance
to their own in full Expectation of our Inability to
counteract them...." **Lambert Cadwalader of New
Jersey, 1787**[58]

- "In this congressional legislature, a bare majority
of votes can enact commercial laws, so that the
representatives of the seven northern states, as they
will have a majority, can by law create the most
oppressive monopoly upon the five southern states,
whose circumstances and productions are essentially different from theirs...." **Richard Henry Lee
of Virginia, 1787**[59]

- "The commerce of America, including our exports,
imports, shipping, manufactures, and fisheries may
be properly considered as forming one interest."
Tench Coxe of Pennsylvania, 1788[60]

- "It has been said, we will have a navigation act, and
be restricted to American bottoms, and that high
freight will be the consequence. We certainly ought
to have a navigation act, and we assuredly ought to
give a preference, though not a monopoly, to our
own shipping." **David Ramsey of South Carolina,
1788**[61]

- "By the sundry regulations of commerce, it will be
in the power of Government not only to collect a
vast revenue for the general benefit of the nation,
but to secure the carrying trade in the hands of citizens in preference to strangers." **Hugh Williamson
of North Carolina, 1788**[62]

The Founders on the Union

- "The general objects of the union are, 1st, to protect us against foreign invasion; 2d, to defend us against internal commotions and insurrections; 3d, to promote the commerce, agriculture, and manufactures, of America. These objects are requisite to make us a safe and happy people, and they cannot be attained without a firm and efficient system of union." **William Richardson Davie of North Carolina, 1788**[63]

- "The general government will have the protection and management of the general interests of the United States. The local and particular interests of the different states are left to their respective legislatures." **James Iredell of North Carolina, 1788**[64]

- "It has been said that this new government was to be considered as an experiment. He really was afraid it would prove a fatal one to our peace and happiness. An experiment! What, risk the loss of political existence on experiment! No, sir; if we are to make experiments, rather let them be such as may do good, but which cannot possibly do any injury to us or our posterity. So far from paving any expectation of success from such experiments, he sincerely believed that, when this new Constitution should be adopted, the sun of the Southern States would set, never to rise again." **Rawlins Lowndes of South Carolina, 1788**[65]

- "For to say that a bad government must be established for fear of anarchy, is in reality, saying that we must kill ourselves for fear of dying." **John Williams of New York, 1788**[66]

- "But in large confederacies, the alarm excited by small and gradual encroachments rarely extends to the distant members, or inspires a general spirit of resistance. When we take a view of the United States, we find them embracing interests as various as their territory is extensive. Their habits, their productions, their resources, and their political and commercial relations, are as different as those of any nation upon earth. A general law, therefore, which might be well calculated for Georgia, might operate most disadvantageously and cruelly upon New York." **George Clinton of New York, 1788**[67]

- "There are certain social principles in human nature, from which we may draw the most solid conclusion with respect to the conduct of individuals and of communities. We love our families more than our neighbors; we love our neighbors more than our countrymen in general. The human affections, like the solar heat, lose their intensity as they depart from the centre [*sic*], and become languid in proportion to the expansion of the circle in which they act. On these principles, the attachment of the individual will be first and forever secured by the state governments: they will be a mutual protection and support.... Can the state governments become insignificant while they have the power of raising money independently, and without control? If they are really useful, if they are calculated to promote the essential interests of the people, they must have their confidence and support. The states can never lose their powers till the whole people of America are robbed of their liberties. These must go together; they must support each other, or meet one common fate." **Alexander Hamilton of New York, 1788**[68]

- "Make the best of this new government—say it is composed by any thing but inspiration—you ought to be extremely cautious, watchful, jealous of your liberty; for, instead of securing your rights, you may lose them forever. If a wrong step be now made, the republic may be lost forever. If this new government will not come up to the expectation of the people, and they shall be disappointed, their liberty will be lost, and tyranny must and will arise. I repeat it again, and I beg gentlemen to consider, that a wrong step, made now, will plunge us into misery, and our republic will be lost." **Patrick Henry of Virginia, 1788**[69]

- "But, notwithstanding this, we are wandering on the great ocean of human affairs. I see no landmark to guide us. We are running we know not whither. Difference of opinion has gone to a degree of inflammatory resentment in different parts of the country, which has been occasioned by this perilous innovation. The federal Convention ought to have amended the old system; for this purpose they were solely delegated; the object of their mission extended to no other consideration." **Patrick Henry of Virginia, 1788**[70]

- "Sir, without a radical alteration, the states will never be embraced in one federal pale. If you attempt to force it down men's throats, and call it union, dreadful consequences must follow." **Patrick Henry of Virginia, 1788**[71]

The Founders on the Powers of the Government Under the Constitution

- "A parallel has been drawn between the British Parliament and Congress. The powers of Congress are all circumscribed, defined, and clearly laid down. So far they may go, but no farther. But, sir, what are the powers of the British Parliament? They have no written constitution in Britain.... The power of Parliament is...unbounded." **Samuel Johnston of North Carolina, 1788**[72]

- "I know it is said that what is not given up to the United States will be retained by the individual states. I know it ought to be so, and should be so understood; but, sir, it is not *declared* to be so.... There ought to be a bill of rights, in order that those in power may not step over the boundary between the powers of government and the rights of the people, which they may do when there is nothing to prevent them.... I look upon it, therefore, that there ought to be something to confine the power of this government within its proper boundaries." **Samuel Spencer of North Carolina, 1788**[73]

- "The powers of Congress are limited and enumerated. We say we have given them those powers, but we do not say we have given them more. We retain all those rights which we have not given away to the general government.... It is as plain a thing as possibly can be, that Congress can have no power but what we expressly give them. There is an express clause [the "Necessary and Proper Clause"] which, however disingenuously it has been perverted from its true meaning, clearly demonstrates that they are confined to those powers which are given them.... This clause specifies that they shall make laws to carry into execution *all the powers vested* by this Constitution; consequently, they can make no laws to execute any other power. This clause gives no new power, but declares that those already given are to be executed by proper laws." **Richard Dobbs Spaight of North Carolina, 1788**[74]

- "The distinction which has been taken between the nature of a federal and state government appeared to be conclusive—that in the former, no powers could be executed, or assumed, but such as were expressly delegated; that in the latter, the indefinite power was given to the government, except on points which were by express compact reserved to the people.... The general government has no powers but what are expressly granted to it; it therefore has no power to take away the liberty of the press. That invaluable blessing, which deserves all the encomiums the gentleman has justly bestowed upon it, is secured by all our state constitutions; and to have mentioned it in our general Constitution would perhaps furnish an argument, hereafter, that the general government had a right to exercise powers not expressly delegated to it." **Charles Pinckney of South Carolina, 1788**[75]

- "The paragraph in question is an absolute decree of the people. The Congress *shall* have power. It does not say that they shall exercise it; but our necessities say they *must*, and the experience of ages say that they will; and finally, when the expenses of the nation, by their ambition, are grown enormous, that they *will* oppress and subject; for, sir, they may lay taxes, duties, imposts, and excises!" **William Symmes Jr. of Massachusetts, 1788**[76]

- "A few years ago, we fought for liberty; we framed a general government on free principles; we placed the state legislatures, in whom the people have a full and a fair representation, between Congress and the people. We were then, it is true, too cautious, and too much restricted the powers of the general government. But now it is proposed to go into the contrary, and a more dangerous extreme—to remove all barriers, to give the new government free access to our pockets, and ample command of our persons, and that without providing for a genuine and fair representation of the people." **Melancton Smith of New York, 1788**[77]

- "The powers of the new government are general, and calculated to embrace the aggregate interests of the Union, and the general interest of each state, so far as it stands in relation to the whole. The object of the state governments is to provide for their internal interests, as unconnected with the United States, and as composed of minute parts or districts. A particular knowledge, therefore, of the local circumstances of any state, as they may vary in different districts, is unnecessary for the federal representative." **Alexander Hamilton of New York, 1788**[78]

- "It is true, the 9th section restrains their power [The States] with respect to certain objects. But these restrictions are very limited, some of them improper, some unimportant, and others not easily understood." **John Williams of New York, 1788**[79]

- "The laws of the United States are supreme, as to all their proper, constitutional objects: the laws of the states are supreme in the same way....I wish the committee to remember that the Constitution under examination is framed upon truly republican principles; and that, as it is expressly designed to provide for the common protection and the general welfare of the United States, it must be utterly repugnant to this Constitution to subvert the state governments, or to oppress the people." **Alexander Hamilton of New York, 1788**[80]

- "Let me, however, call it [the Union] by another name—a representative federal republic, as contra-distinguished from a confederacy. The former is more wisely constructed than the latter; it places the remedy in the hands which *feel* the disorder: the other places the remedy in those hands which *cause* the disorder. The evils that are most complained of in such governments (and with justice) are faction, dissension, and consequent subjection of the majority, who, instead of consulting the interest of the whole community collectively, attend some-times to partial and local advantages." **Francis Corbin of Virginia, 1788**[81]

- "I shall be told in this place that those who are to tax us are our representatives. To this I answer, that there is no real check to prevent their ruining us. There is no actual responsibility. The only semblance of a check is the negative power of not reelecting them. This, sir, is but a feeble barrier, when their personal interest, their ambition and avarice, come to be put in contrast with the happiness of the people. All checks founded on any thing but self-love will not avail. The Constitution reflects in the most degrading and mortifying manner on the virtue, integrity, and wisdom of the state legislatures; it presupposes that the chosen few who go to Congress will have more upright hearts, and more enlightened minds, than those who are members of the individual legislatures. To suppose that ten gentlemen shall have more real, substantial merit than one hundred and seventy, is humiliating to the last degree.... Nothing is more perilous than constructive power, which gentlemen are so willing to trust their happiness to." **Patrick Henry of Virginia, 1788**[82]

- "There have been no instances shown of a voluntary cession of power, sufficient to induce me to grant the most dangerous power; a possibility of their future relinquishment will not persuade me to yield such powers." **Patrick Henry of Virginia, 1788**[83]

- "When a question arises with respect to the legality of any power, exercised or assumed by Congress, it is plain on the side of the governed: *Is it enumerated in the Constitution?* If it be, it is legal and just. It is otherwise arbitrary and unconstitutional." **Henry Lee of Virginia, 1788**[84]

Appendix B

Several hundred proposed constitutional amendments circulated the United States in the month leading to ratification. James Madison reduced the list to twelve, and ten were ratified in 1791. The Twenty-seventh Amendment was also part of the original twelve. Listed below are several interesting amendments that never made it to Madison's final dozen. Several would have limited the power of the judiciary, while others were aimed at curtailing the powers of Congress or elected officials in general. Two, one from Maryland and one from Virginia, were in essence secession amendments. If Americans are serious about amending the Constitution—and thirty-two states are on the record as favoring a constitutional convention to amend the Constitution—these, along with Professor Kevin Gutzman's "Federalism Amendment,"[1] would be a good place to start.

Proposed Amendments

"*Resolved*, That no person shall be eligible as a senator for more than six years in any term of twelve years, and that it shall be in the power of the legislatures of the several states to recall their senators, or either of them, and to elect others in their stead, to serve for the remainder of the time for which such senator or senators, so recalled, were appointed." **Proposed by Melancton Smith of New York, 1788.**[2]

"*Resolved*, as the opinion of this committee, that nothing in the Constitution, now under consideration, shall be construed to authorize the Congress to make or alter *any regulations*, in any state, respecting the times, places, or manner of holding elections for senators or representatives, unless the legislature of such state shall neglect or refuse to make laws or regulate ones for the purpose, or, from any circumstance, be incapable of making the same, and then only until the legislature of such state shall make provision in the premises." **Proposed by Samuel Jones of New York, 1788.**[3]

"*Provided*, That no money be borrowed on the credit of the United States, without the assent of two thirds of the members of both houses present." **Proposed by John Lansing of New York, 1788.**[4]

"*Resolved*, as the opinion of the committee, that the power of Congress to establish post-offices and post-roads is not to be construed to extend to the laying out, making, altering, or repairing highways, in any state, without the consent of the legislature of such state." **Proposed by Samuel Jones of New York, 1788.**[5]

From Virginia's Proposed Bill of Rights[6]

"2ᵈ. That all power is naturally invested in, and consequently derived from, the people; that magistrates therefore are their *trustees* and *agents*, at all times amendable to them."

"3ᵈ. That government ought to be instituted for the common benefit, protection, and security of the people; and that the doctrine of non-resistance against arbitrary power and oppression is absurd, slavish, and destructive to the good and happiness of mankind."

"4ᵗʰ. That no man or set of men are entitled to separate or exclusive public emoluments or privileges from the community, but in consideration of public services, which not being descendible, neither ought the offices of magistrate, legislator, or judge, or any other public office, to be hereditary."

"5ᵗʰ. That the legislative, executive, and judicial powers of government should be separate and distinct; and, that the members of the two first may be restrained from oppression by feeling and participating the public burdens, they should, at fixed periods, be reduced to a private station, return into the mass of the people, and the vacancies be supplied by certain and regular elections, in which all or any part of the former members to be eligible or ineligible, as the rules of the Constitution of government, and the laws, shall direct."

From Virginia's Proposed Amendments to the Constitution[7]

"7ᵗʰ. That no commercial treaty shall be ratified without the concurrence of two thirds of the whole number of the members of the Senate; and no treaty ceding, contracting, restraining, or suspending, the territorial rights or claims to fishing in the American seas, or navigation of the American rivers, shall be made, but in cases of the most urgent and extreme necessity; nor shall any such treaty be ratified without the concurrence of three fourths of the whole number of the members of both houses respectively."

"8th. That no navigation law, or law regulating commerce, shall be passed without the consent of two thirds of the members present, in both houses."

"9th. That no standing army, or regular troops, shall be raised, or kept up, in time of peace, without the consent of two thirds of the members present, in both houses."

"14th. That the judicial power of the United States shall be vested in one Supreme Court, and in such courts of admiralty as Congress may from time to time ordain and establish in any of the different states. The judicial power shall extend to all cases in law and equity arising under treaties made, or which shall be made, under the authority of the United States; to all cases affecting ambassadors, other foreign ministers, and consuls; to all cases of admiralty and maritime jurisdiction; to controversies to which the United States shall be a party; to controversies between two or more states, and between parties claiming land under the grants of different states. In all cases affecting ambassadors, other foreign ministers, and consuls, and those in which a state shall be a party, the Supreme Court shall have original jurisdiction; in all other cases before mentioned, the Supreme Court shall have appellate jurisdiction, as to matters of law only, except in cases of equity, and of admiralty, and maritime jurisdiction, in which the Supreme Court shall have appellate jurisdiction both as to law and fact, with such exceptions and under such regulations as the Congress shall make: but the judicial power of the United States shall extend to no case where the cause of action shall have originated before the ratification of the Constitution, except in disputes between states about their territory, disputes between persons claiming lands under the grants of different states, and suits for debts due to the United States."

"16th. That Congress shall not alter, modify, or interfere in the times, places, or manner of holding elections for senators or representatives, or either of them, except when the legislature of any state shall neglect, refuse, or be disabled, by invasion or rebellion, to prescribe the same."

"17th. That those clauses which declare that Congress shall not exercise certain powers, be not interpreted, in any manner whatsoever, to extend the powers of Congress; but that they be construed either as making exceptions to the specified powers where this shall be the case, or otherwise, as inserted merely for greater caution."

From Maryland (this amendment was rejected in the Maryland Ratifying Convention but is similar to Virginia's 3rd proposal in its Bill of Rights)

"15. That it be declared, that all persons intrusted [*sic*] with the legislative or executive powers of government are trustees and servants of the public; and, as such, accountable for their conduct. Wherefore, whenever the ends of government are perverted, and public liberty manifestly endangered, and all other means of redress are ineffectual, the people may, and of right ought to, reform the old, or establish a new government. The doctrine of non-resistance against arbitrary power and oppression is absurd, slavish, and destructive of the good and happiness of mankind."[8]

From the Massachusetts Ratifying Convention

"*Fifthly*. That Congress erect no company with exclusive advantages of commerce."[9]

From the Pennsylvania Dissent of the Minority

"14. That the judiciary power of the United States shall be confined to cases affecting ambassadors, other public ministers and consuls; to cases of admiralty and maritime jurisdiction; to controversies to which the United States shall be a party; to controversies between two or more states—between a state and citizens of different states—between citizens claiming lands under grants of different states; and between a state or the citizens thereof and foreign states, and in criminal cases, to such only as are expressly enumerated in the constitution, and that the United States in Congress assembled shall not have power to enact laws, which shall alter the laws of descents and distribution of the effects of deceased persons, the titles of lands or goods, or the regulation of contracts in the individual states."[10]

Acknowledgments

This book would not have been possible without the support and encouragement of my wife Samantha. She has dutifully waded through another round of deadlines while taking care of hearth and home. No words can express my gratitude. The library staff at Chattahoochee Valley Community College, most importantly Xueying Chen and Cory Williams, provided research assistance and helped secure the many volumes of information needed for this work. As usual, they went above and beyond the call of duty. I would also like to thank Clyde N. Wilson for his outstanding critique of the original manuscript. His advice is always top notch. Tom Woods, Kevin Gutzman, Jeff Rogers, Marshall DeRosa, Don Livingston, and Bart Talbert provided insight and comments to improve the work. Finally, I would like to thank my children and my students for giving me the inspiration to write this book. This work is for you and the many future generations of Americans who will benefit from learning the true intent of the Constitution. America cannot survive without you. Please take heed.

Notes

Introduction

1. Catherine Drinker Bowen, *Miracle at Philadelphia: The Story of the Constitutional Convention May to September 1787* (Boston: Little, Brown and Co., 1986).

2. Video available at http://www.breitbart.tv/liberal-star-blogger-ezra-klein-constitution-has-no-binding-power-on-anything-confusing-because-its-over-100-years-old/ (accessed March 21, 2011).

3. Ron Chernow, "The Founding Fathers Versus the Tea Party," September 23, 2010, http://www.nytimes.com/2010/09/24/opinion/24chernow.html (accessed March 21, 2011).

4. *Annals of Congress*, 1st Congress, 1st Session, 759.

Chapter 1

1.   Jonathan Elliot, ed., *The Debates in the Several State Conventions on the Adoption of the Federal Constitution as Recommended by the General Convention at Philadelphia in 1787* (New York, NY: Burt Franklin Reprints, 1974), V: 129. Hereafter referred to as DAFC.

2.   Ibid., III: 22.

3.   Merrill Jensen, et. al., ed., *The Documentary History of the Ratification of the Constitution* (Madison, WI: State Historical Society of Wisconsin, 1976-2010), II: 393. Hereafter referred to as *Documentary History*.

4.   Ibid., XIV: 333.

5.   Ibid., XVI: 74.

6.   Ibid., II: 384.

7.   Ibid., IX: 661.

8.   *DAFC*, III: 28.

9.   Ibid., II: 209-210.

10.   Max Farrand, ed., *The Records of the Federal Convention of 1787* (New Haven: Yale University Press, 1937, 1966), IV: 84. Hereafter referred to as Farrand.

11.   Ibid., III: 518.

Chapter 2

1.   *DAFC*, IV: 21.

2.   Ibid., V: 136.

3.   Ibid., II: 304.

4.   Ibid., V: 555.

5.   Ibid., II: 242.

6.   *Documentary History*, XIV: 185.

7.   Ibid., II: 631-632.

8.   *DAFC*, II: 36.

9.   Ibid., 37-38.

10.   Ibid., 442.

11.   *Documentary History*, XVI: 157.

12.   *DAFC*, II: 427.

13. Ibid., I: 338.
14. *Documentary History,* XVI: 232-233.
15. *DAFC,* V: 137-138.
16. Ibid., V: 166.
17. Ibid., 168.
18. Ibid., 170.
19. *Documentary History,* XVI: 233-234.
20. Ibid., XVI: 234.
21. Ibid., XVI: 51.
22. *DAFC,* II: 305.
23. *Documentary History,* X: 1292.
24. *DAFC,* II: 306.
25. *Documentary History,* XVI: 311.
26. *DAFC,* V: 169.
27. *Documentary History,* XVI: 296.
28. *DAFC,* V: 377.
29. Ibid., 401.
30. Ibid.
31. Ibid., 402.
32. Ibid.
33. Walter Hartwell Bennett, ed., *Letters From the Federal Farmer to the Republican* (Tuscaloosa, AL: University of Alabama Press, 1978), 15; The authorship of the Letters has long been an issue of historical controversy. For a quick summary of the principle contenders, see Brion McClanahan, *The Politically Incorrect Guide to the Founding Fathers* (Washington, DC: Regnery Publishing, Inc., 2009), 264.
34. *Documentary History,* IV: 169-170.
35. Ibid., XIV: 302.
36. Ibid., XV: 299.
37. *DAFC,* II: 30.
38. Ibid., III: 60.
39. Ibid., II: 325.
40. Ibid., IV: 51.
41. Ibid., 441.
42. *Documentary History,* XVI: 186.

43. Charles R. King, ed. *The Life and Correspondence of Rufus King* (New York: G.P. Putnum's Sons, 1894-1900), I: 305.

44. *DAFC*, II: 49.

45. Ibid., IV: 249.

46. *Annals of Congress*, 1st Congress, 1st Session, 797-802.

47. *DAFC*, IV: 50, 58.

48. *Documentary History*, XVI: 187.

49. *DAFC*, V: 184-185.

50. Ibid., 226-228.

51. Ibid., 425-427.

52. Ibid., 228, 425-427.

53. *Documentary History*, IV: 413.

54. Ibid., VI: 1449.

55. Ibid., 1408.

56. Ibid., 1284.

57. Ibid., X: 1261.

58. *DAFC*, V: 377.

59. Ibid., 394.

60. Ibid., 418.

61. Ibid., 419.

62. Ibid., II: 92-93.

63. Ibid., III: 377-378.

64. Ibid., V: 127.

65. Ibid., 469; 476-477.

66. Ibid., 161.

67. *Documentary History*, XVI: 22.

68. Ibid., XIX: 167.

69. Ibid., 470.

70. Ibid., VI: 1311.

71. Ibid., XIV: 264.

72. *Documentary History*, XV: 425.

73. *Annals of Congress*, 1st Congress, 3rd Session, 1945-1946.

74. *DAFC*, II: 350.

75. Ibid., V: 433.

76. Bennett, ed., *Letters From the Federal Farmer*, 19-20.

77. *Documentary History*, XIV: 424-425.

78. Ibid., XIX: 470.

79. *DAFC*, IV: 75.

80. Ibid., II: 57.

81. Ibid., 60.

82. Ibid., 62.

83. Ibid., 468.

84. Ibid., 191.

85. Ibid., IV: 81-82.

86. *Documentary History*, XIV: 216.

87. *DAFC*, V: 434-435.

88. Ibid.

89. *Documentary History*, XV: 378-379.

90. Ibid., XIII: 279-280.

91. Ibid., III: 141.

92. Ibid., 402.

93. Ibid., X: 1773.

94. Ibid., XIV: 361-362.

95. Ibid., 264.

96. Ibid., XV: 335-336.

97. Ibid., XIV: 325.

98. Ibid., XVI: 25.

99. Ibid., X: 1773.

100. Farrand, III: 547.

101. *Documentary History*, XV: 430.

102. Ibid., XIV: 213-214.

103. *DAFC*, II: 350.

104. Ibid., V: 461.

105. Ibid., 489-490.

106. Ibid.

107. Ibid., III: 604.

108. Farrand, II: 504.

109. Ibid., 529-530.

110. *DAFC*, V: 543-544.

111. Ibid., 544.

112.   *Documentary History*, XV: 433; 479.

113.   Ibid., 458.

114.   Ibid., 510.

115.   Farrand, III: 363-364.

116.   Ibid., 375-376.

117.   Ibid., II: 318-319.; *DAFC*, V: 131.

118.   *Documentary History*, XV: 236.

119.   Ibid., 419.

120.   James Curtis Ballagh, ed., *The Letters of Richard Henry Lee* (New York: Macmillan Co., 1911-1914), II: 237.

121.   Farrand, II: 329, 509, 616.

122.   *Documentary History*, II: 169.

123.   Bennett, ed., Letters, 21.

124.   *Documentary History*, II: 197.

125.   Ibid., XIV: 263.

126.   Ibid., 145-146.

127.   *DAFC*, II: 521.

128.   *Documentary History*, XV: 62.

129.   Ibid., 68.

130.   Ibid., 395.

131.   *DAFC*, II: 97.

132.   Ibid., IV: 99.

133.   Ibid., III: 380-381.

134.   Ibid., V: 139-140.

135.   Farrand, I: 245-246.

136.   Ibid., II: 316-317.

137.   Ibid., 331-332.

138.   Ibid., 332.

139.   Ibid., 385-386.

140.   Ibid., 386-388.

141.   *Documentary History*, XIV: 290-291.

142.   Ibid., 301.

143.   *DAFC*, II: 521-522.

144.   *Documentary History*, XV: 318-319.

145.   Ibid., 320-321.

146. *DAFC*, II: 197.

147. Farrand, II: 640.

148. *Documentary History*, XIII: 199.

149. Ibid., III: 167-168.

150. Bennet, ed., *Letters*, 27.

151. *Documentary History*, XIII: 402-403.

152. Ibid., 413-416.

153. *DAFC*, II: 468.

154. Ibid., III: 206-207.

155. Ibid., IV: 161-162.

156. *Documentary History*, XV: 220.

157. Ibid., 472-473.

158. Ibid., XVI: 379-380.

159. *DAFC*, III: 443.

160. *Documentary History*, XIV: 218-220.

161. Ibid., XV: 249.

162. *DAFC*, II: 190.

163. Ferrand, III: 99.

Chapter 3

1. *DAFC*, V: 128, 131, 192.

2. Ibid., 140.

3. Ibid.

4. Ibid., 141.

5. Farrand, I: 71.

6. Ibid., 96.

7. Ibid., 97.

8. Ibid., IV: 17–18.

9. *Documentary History*, VIII: 44.

10. Ibid., XIV: 9-10.

11. Ibid., XIII: 542–43.

12. *DAFC*, II: 480.

13. *Documentary History*, XVI: 396–97.

14. *DAFC*, V: 205.

15. Ibid., IV: 104.
16. Farrand, II: 33.
17. Ibid., 33–35.
18. Ibid., 34–36.
19. Ibid., 54.
20. Ibid., 54–55.
21. Ibid., 102.
22. *Documentary History*, XVI: 500.
23. Ibid., XV: 133.
24. Ibid., XIII: 335.
25. *DAFC*, III: 483-484.
26. *Documentary History*, XV: 280.
27. Ibid., XVI: 422.
28. Ibid., 496.
29. Ibid.
30. Farrand, I: 85.
31. Ibid., II: 64.
32. Ibid., 65.
33. Ibid., 66.
34. Ibid., 68.
35. *Documentary History*, XVII: 125.
36. Ibid., 13.
37. *Documentary History*, XV: 525.
38. Ibid., XVI: 322.
39. Ibid., XV: 496–97.
40. Farrand, II: 65–69.
41. *DAFC*, III: 500.
42. Michael Likosky, "Obama: Recession Could Delay Rescinding Bush Tax Cuts," *Huffington Post*, September 7, 2008, http://www.huffington post.com/2008/09/07/obama-recession-could-del_n_124647.html (accessed June 6, 2011).
43. Justin Fox, "Barack Obama won't raise your taxes. At least not in 2009," Time.com, November 6, 2008, http://curiouscapitalist.blogs.time. com/2008/11/06/barack-obama-wont-raise-your-taxes-at-least-not-in-2009/ (accessed June 6, 2011).

44. *DAFC*, V: 140–41.
45. Ibid., V: 140.
46. *Documentary History*, XV: 495.
47. *DAFC*, II: 408.
48. Ibid., IV: 114.
49. Ibid., III: 496.
50. Ibid., IV: 107–8.
51. Ibid., II: 497.
52. *Documentary History*, XVI: 479.
53. *DAFC*, III: 497-498.
54. Farrand, I: 119–20.
55. Ibid., II: 41.
56. Ibid., 42-43.
57. Ibid., 392.
58. *DAFC*, III: 499.
59. Ibid., IV: 118.
60. *Documentary History*, XVII: 68.
61. *DAFC*, IV: 119–20.
62. Ibid., 125.
63. Ibid., III: 499.
64. Ibid., 509–10.
65. John P. Foley, ed., *The Jefferson Cyclopedia* (New York: Funk and Wagnalls, 1900), 879.
66. *Documentary History*, XVII: 309-310.
67. Farrand, I: 98.
68. Ibid., 98-99.
69. Ibid., 100-101.
70. Ibid., 101-103.
71. Ibid., 99-100, 104.
72. *Documentary History*, II: 211–12.
73. Ibid., 505.
74. Ibid., XV: 375–76.
75. *DAFC*, IV: 214.
76. *Documentary History*, X: 1611.
77. *DAFC*, IV: 473.

78. *Documentary History*, XVI: 448, 450–51.
79. *DAFC*, IV: 75.
80. For a detailed analysis of the abuse of executive orders and signing statements, see Thomas E. Woods Jr., and Kevin R.C. Gutzman, *Who Killed the Constitution* (New York: Three Rivers Press, 2008), 185–97.
81. Farrand, II: 29–31.
82. Ibid., 112.
83. Ibid., I: 80.
84. Ibid., II: 119.
85. *Documentary History*, XVI: 387–90.

Chapter 4

1. Farrand, I: 21.
2. Ibid., 124.
3. Ibid.
4. Ibid., 125.
5. Ibid., II: 45–46.
6. Ibid., 429.
7. Bennett, ed., *Letters*, 100.
8. *Documentary History*, XVI: 431–32.
9. Ibid., XVIII: 88-89.
10. Foley, ed., *Jefferson Cyclopedia*, 478.
11. Ibid., 844.
12. Farrand, I: 97–101.
13. *DAFC*, V: 429.
14. Ibid., 483.
15. Ibid., II: 489.
16. Ibid., 196.
17. Ibid., IV: 156–57.
18. Ibid., III: 539–41.
19. Ibid., 553.
20. Ibid., 554.
21. Ibid., 521–22, 527.
22. *Documentary History*, XVI: 120–22.

23. *DAFC*, V: 468.
24. Farrand, II: 27.
25. *DAFC*, V: 468.
26. Ibid., III: 554.
27. Appendix B.
28. *DAFC*, IV: 160.
29. Ibid., 163.

Chapter 5

1. Farrand, II: 447–48.
2. Ibid., 637.
3. *Documentary History*, XVII: 274.
4. *Statutes at Large*, 1ˢᵗ Congress, 1ˢᵗ Session, 50–53.
5. Ibid., 454.
6. Foley, ed., *Jefferson Cyclopedia*, 510.
7. Jared Sparks, ed., *The Life of Gouverneur Morris with Selections from His Correspondence and Miscellaneous Papers* (Boston: Gray and Bowen), III: 192.
8. *Jefferson Cyclopedia*, 513.
9. *Documentary History*, XIV: 115.
10. E.H. Scott, ed., *The Federalist and Other Contemporary Papers on the Constitution of the United States* (Chicago: Scott, Foresman and Company, 1894), 764–65.
11. *DAFC*, III: 90.
12. *Documentary History*, XIV: 415.
13. Quoted in Forrest McDonald, *The Presidency of George Washington* (Lawrence, KS: University Press of Kansas, 1974), 147. McDonald provides a concise history of the event on pages 145–47.
14. William Findely, *History of the Insurrection in the Four Western Counties of Pennsylvania in the Year 1794* (Philadelphia: Samuel Harrison Smith, 1796).
15. Farrand, II: 316.
16. Christopher G. Browning Jr., Solicitor General of the state of North Carolina, to Roy Cooper, Attorney General of the state of North Carolina,

memorandum, February 23, 2011, http://www.ncdoj.gov/
getdoc/99ceb50b-50bb-48da-b9b5-64194b26c315/House-Bill-2-letter-
memo.aspx (accessed June 6, 2011).

17.   Farrand, II: 28–29, 389.

18.   Bennett, ed., *Letters*, 26.

19.   *Documentary History*, XIV: 14.

20.   Ibid., 345.

21.   Ibid., XV: 23.

22.   Ibid., 453.

23.   Ibid., IX: 1158.

24.   *DAFC*, IV: 179.

25.   Ibid., II: 353, 355–56.

26.   Ibid., 362.

27.   *Documentary History*, XV: 222.

28.   Ibid., 479.

29.   Ibid., 493.

30.   Ibid., 200.

31.   Ibid., II: 416.

32.   *DAFC*, IV: 179.

33.   *Documentary History*, XIV: 387.

34.   Ibid., 66.

35.   *DAFC*, IV: 540.

36.   Ibid., 528.

37.   See Thomas E. Woods Jr., *Nullification* (Washington, DC: Regnery
       Publishing, Inc., 2010) for the most recent and concise synopsis of the
       arguments surrounding nullification.

38.   *DAFC*, V: 552.

39.   Ibid., V: 226.

40.   Farrand, II: 332.

41.   *DAFC*, IV: 24.

42.   Ibid., V: 308.

43.   Ibid., 303.

44.   Ibid., 206–7.

45.   Farrand., II: 475.

46.   Ibid., 469.

47. *DAFC*, V: 555-556.
48. *Documentary History*, XV: 129.
49. Ibid., 421.
50. Ibid., XIII: 57–59.
51. Farrand, I: 445.
52. *Documentary History*, XIII: 418–19.
53. *DAFC*, III: 161.
54. Richardson, *Messages and Papers*, I.

Chapter 6

1. *Documentary History*, I.
2. Farrand, II: 587–88, 633, 637.
3. *Documentary History*, XVI: 455.
4. Ibid., XVI: 350.
5. *DAFC*, II: 403.
6. Ibid., 159–60.
7. *Documentary History*, XVI: 202.
8. *DAFC*, II: 93.
9. Ibid., 436.
10. *Documentary History*, XVIII: 130.
11. *DAFC*, II: 177, 406.
12. Ibid., IV: 244, III: 659.
13. *Documentary History*, XV: 19.
14. *DAFC*, II: 550.
15. *Annals of Congress*, 1ˢᵗ Session, 1ˢᵗ Congress: 456.
16. *DAFC*, III: 659; IV: 244.
17. Ibid., II: 44, 148–49, 119.
18. Ibid., IV: 191–200.
19. *Annals of Congress*, 1ˢᵗ Session, 1ˢᵗ Congress: 758–59.
20. See for example Brion McClanahan, "Religion and the Founding Generation," http://www.humanevents.com/article.php?id=39340 Retrieved on March 10, 2011.
21. *Documentary History*, XIV: 11.
22. Bennett, ed., *Letters*, 112.

23. *DAFC*, II: 111.
24. *Documentary History*, XV: 28.
25. Bennett, ed., *Letters*, 29.
26. *Documentary History*, XVI: 9.
27. Ibid., XVIII: 126.
28. *DAFC*, IV: 145.
29. Ibid., II: 551.
30. *DAFC*, III: 659; IV: 244.
31. *Documentary History*, II: 624.
32. *DAFC*, II: 406.
33. Ibid., 552.
34. Ibid., III: 425.
35. *DAFC*, III: 411.
36. Annals, I: 781.
37. *Documentary History*, XV: 445.
38. *DAFC*, IV: 176–77.
39. Ibid., III: 50.
40. *Documentary History*, XVI: 56.

Appendix A

1. *Documentary History*, III: 164.
2. Farrand, I: 90.
3. *DAFC*, II: 93.
4. Ibid., IV: 34.
5. Ibid., IV: 15–16.
6. Ibid., 58.
7. Ibid., 287.
8. Ibid., 313.
9. Ibid., II: 69.
10. Ibid., 217; 220.
11. Ibid., 224.
12. Ibid., 239.
13. Ibid.. 241.
14. Ibid., 319.

15. Ibid., 334.
16. Ibid., III: 30.
17. Ibid., 40.
18. Ibid., 171.
19. Ibid., 180.
20. Ibid., V, 136.
21. Ibid.
22. Ibid., 137.
23. Ibid., 163.
24. Ibid.
25. Ibid., 269.
26. Ibid., II, 202.
27. Ibid., 209–10.
28. Ibid., IV: 257.
29. Ibid., II: 229.
30. Ibid., 387.
31. Ibid., III: 31–32.
32. Ibid., 137.
33. Ibid., II: 20–21.
34. Ibid., 5.
35. Ibid., 6.
36. Ibid., 305–6.
37. Ibid., 310.
38. *Documentary History*, II: 395–96.
39. Ibid., IX: 924.
40. Ibid., VIII: 440.
41. *DAFC*, II: 46.
42. Ibid., 257.
43. Ibid., 283.
44. Ibid., 289.
45. Ibid., 298.
46. Ibid., IV: 123, 43.
47. Ibid., 133, 38.
48. *Documentary History*, X: 1353–54.
49. Farrand, II: 635–36; see also *Documentary History*, IV: 14.

50.   *Documentary History*, IV: 289.

51.   Ibid., V: 723.

52.   Ibid., VIII: 81.

53.   Ibid., XIV: 82.

54.   Ibid., 154.

55.   Ibid., 92–93; 141.

56.   Ibid., 213–14.

57.   Ibid., XIII: 359.

58.   Ibid., 353.

59.   Ibid., XIV: 369.

60.   Ibid., XV: 169.

61.   Ibid., XVI: 24.

62.   Ibid., 204–5.

63.   *DAFC*, IV: 17.

64.   Ibid., 38.

65.   Ibid., 271–72.

66.   Ibid., II: 243.

67.   Ibid., 262.

68.   Ibid., 354–55.

69.   Ibid, III: 22.

70.   Ibid., 23.

71.   Ibid., 159.

72.   Ibid., IV: 64.

73.   Ibid., 137.

74.   Ibid., 141.

75.   Ibid., 259–60; 315–16.

76.   Ibid., II: 72.

77.   Ibid., 250.

78.   Ibid., 265.

79.   Ibid., 330.

80.   Ibid., 356.

81.   Ibid., III: 107.

82.   Ibid., 167.

83.   Ibid., 169.

84.   Ibid., 186.

Appendix B

1. Kevin Gutzman, et al., "The Federal Solution for a Federal Crisis," http://kevingutzman.com/articles/assets/ArticleVConvention_04212010.pdf (accessed June 7, 2011).
2. *DAFC*, II: 289.
3. Ibid., 325–26.
4. Ibid., 406.
5. Ibid.
6. Ibid., III: 657–59.
7. Ibid., 659–61.
8. Ibid., II: 553.
9. Ibid., 177.
10. *Documentary History*, II: 625.

INDEX